FIRST THINGS FIRST

A WORLD BANK PUBLICATION

FIRST THINGS FIRST
MEETING BASIC HUMAN NEEDS
IN THE DEVELOPING COUNTRIES

Paul Streeten

with
Shahid Javed Burki
Mahbub ul Haq
Norman Hicks
Frances Stewart

PUBLISHED FOR THE WORLD BANK
OXFORD UNIVERSITY PRESS

Oxford University Press

NEW YORK OXFORD LONDON GLASGOW
TORONTO MELBOURNE WELLINGTON HONG KONG
TOKYO KUALA LUMPUR SINGAPORE JAKARTA
DELHI BOMBAY CALCUTTA MADRAS KARACHI
NAIROBI DAR ES SALAAM CAPE TOWN

Library of Congress Cataloging in Publication Data

Streeten, Paul
  First things first.
  Bibliography: p. 193
  Includes index.
  1. Underdeveloped areas—Economic policy.
2. Economic assistance. I. World Bank. II. Title.
HC59.7.S859   338.9'009172'4   81-16836
ISBN 0-19-520368-2   AACR2
ISBN 0-19-520369-0 (pbk.)

Contents

Foreword

Judged by the usual yardsticks of economic growth, the development process of the past three decades was a spectacular, unprecedented, and unexpected success: it resulted in an annual increase of more than 3 percent in income per head in the developing world. Judged by even the normal measures of social development, the development process must also be labeled a success. Life expectancy at birth increased from only forty-two years in 1950 to nearly sixty years in 1980. But judged by the reduction of poverty, it was far less successful. The aggregate statistics quoted above hide tremendous disparities between nations and within nations. Overall economic growth and social progress did not mean much improvement in the circumstances of the poorer segments of the population. By World Bank calculations, even now some 750 million people live below a nutritionally defined poverty line. This is nearly one-third of the combined population of the developing countries.

Must such a large number of people be condemned forever to live in absolute poverty?

This book is about one possible approach to helping the poor emerge from their poverty. It is about an approach that enables the poor to earn or obtain their "basic needs."

The emphasis on basic needs heightens concern with meeting the consumption needs of the entire population, not only in the customary areas of education and health, but also in nutrition, housing, water supply, and sanitation. In formulating policies aimed at reducing poverty, a good deal of attention has been paid in the economic literature to restructuring patterns of production and income so that they benefit the poor. But similar attention has not been devoted to the consumption side. This imbalance is restored if the basic needs objective is placed at the center of the development dialogue where it belongs.

It is true that the only way absolute poverty can ᵥe eliminated, on a permanent and sustainable basis, is to increase the productivity of the poor. But direct methods to increase the productivity of the poor need to be supplemented with efforts to provide their unmet basic needs, for at least the following four reasons:

—First, education and health are required—in addition to machines, land, and credit—to increase productivity. Sufficient empirical evidence is now available to suggest that education and health services often make a greater contribution to improving labor productivity than do most alternative investments.

—Second, many poor people have no physical assets—neither a small farm nor a small industry. They are the landless or urban poor. The only asset they possess is their own two hands and their willingness to work. In such a situation the best investment is in human resource development.

—Third, it is not enough to enable the poor to earn a reasonable income. They also need goods and services on which to spend their income. Markets do not always supply wage goods, particularly public services. Greater production of wage goods and the expansion and redistribution of public services become essential if basic needs of the majority of the population are to be met.

—Finally, it may take a long time to increase the productivity of the absolute poor to a level at which they can afford at least the minimum bundle of basic needs for a productive life. In the interim, some income groups—particularly the bottom 10 to 20 percent—may need short-term subsidy programs.

The emphasis on basic needs, therefore, is a logical step along the path of development thinking. Unfortunately, the term "basic needs" has evoked emotions that have little to do with the meaning that lies behind it. To some, the concept of providing for the basic needs of the poorest represents a futile attempt to redistribute income and provide welfare services to the poor, without stimulating corresponding increases in their productivity to pay for them. To others, it conjures up the image of a move toward socialism, and whispered references are made to the experience of China and Cuba. Yet still others see it as a capitalist conspiracy to deny industrialization and modernization to the developing countries and thereby to keep them dependent on the developed world. It is amazing how two such innocent, five-letter words could mean so many different things to so many different people.

It is possible that "basic needs" has become such a code word that it is impossible to restore a meaningful perspective on this issue without abandoning the code word itself. That should not be too much of a loss. What needs to be protected is the objective, not the word. Emphasis on basic needs must be seen as a pragmatic response to the urgent problem of world poverty; as the ultimate objective of economic development, it should shape national planning for investment, production, and consumption.

To provide the concept of basic needs with an operational meaning—to put some flesh on what was till then an abstraction—some of us in the World Bank undertook extensive work in this area. It was our hope that by drawing on actual country and project experience, by learning from successes as well as from failures, we would be able to design realistic strategies to improve the lot of the absolute poor. We also hoped to separate the real concept of basic needs from several unfortunate interpretations. Whether we succeeded in these objectives will be the test of this book.

It is a great tribute to the vision of Robert S. McNamara that he gave enthusiastic support to this work, which was undertaken in the three years from 1978 to 1980. His tough questioning of all operational work, combined with his compassion and sympathy for the basic objective, were an inspiration and a shield against any muddled thinking.

There were too many people involved in this enterprise to be thanked individually. A partial list appears in the preface. The central figure, however, was Paul Streeten. I entrusted the coordination of the World Bank studies on this subject to his direction in early 1978. His enthusiasm, energy, intellectual compassion, ability to stick to the fundamentals, and willingness to modify the details were the essential driving force around which this book gradually took shape. Our objective was to produce a thoughtful analysis of the basic needs concept and to make the concept more operational for policymakers. I believe that Paul Streeten has succeeded handsomely in this task. He was ably assisted in this by my colleagues Shahid Javed Burki, Norman Hicks, and Frances Stewart. I consider myself honored to be included as one of the authors, though my personal contribution has been rather limited compared with those of my colleagues.

This is not just another book on basic needs. It is a distinct contribution, based on the distillation of an intense dialogue within the World Bank and on actual country experience compiled by the Bank staff. Its appearance at this time should make a valuable contribution to the international debate on this subject.

MAHBUB UL HAQ
*Director, Policy Planning
and Program Review
The World Bank*

Preface

This book attempts to distill the lessons of the World Bank's work on basic needs that started early in 1978. The selection and interpretation of this work is a subjective process, and I do not expect that all those who contributed would agree with everything I say. I have tried to distinguish the result of the work by staff members from my personal interpretation. In chapters 5 and 6 I summarize the work of the Bank staff, whereas in chapter 7 I introduce a more personal element. In any case, the opinions expressed are mine and must not necessarily be attributed to the World Bank.

My debt to others is great. Above all, Mahbub ul Haq has inspired the approach and has contributed constant encouragement, constructive criticisms, and ideas. Hollis Chenery's skepticism has been throughout a healthy influence. Parts of the book owe much to the work of Shahid Javed Burki, Norman Hicks, Akbar Noman, and Frances Stewart. Chapter 3 is an edited version of a paper Norman Hicks and I wrote jointly.

I have also received helpful comments on some parts of earlier drafts from Bela Balassa, Robert Cassen, Paul Isenman, Richard Jolly, and T. N. Srinivasan. Sandra Copp typed numerous versions of the manuscripts and I am very grateful to her.

The book also draws upon the work of the following staff and consultants of the World Bank: Heinz Bachmann, Michael Beenstock, Alan Berg, Gilbert Brown, Richard Cash, Anthony Churchill, David Davies, John Fei, Aklilu Habte, Wadi Haddad, Khalid Ikram, Paul Isenman, John Kalbermatten, Peter Knight, James Koch, Ricardo Moran, Abdun Noor, Selcuk Ozgediz, Gustav Ranis, and Peter Timmer.

Jane H. Carroll edited the manuscript, and Josefina G. Valeriano verified the references. S. A. D. Subasinghe prepared the figures, Brian J. Svikhart designed the book and supervised production, and Joyce Eisen designed the cover. Diana Regenthal read proof of the book, and Winfield Swanson prepared the index.

PAUL STREETEN

FIRST THINGS FIRST

Introduction and Summary

EARLY IN 1978 a World Bank-wide work program was launched to study the operational implications of meeting basic needs within a short period, say, one generation, as a principal objective of national development efforts. This book attempts to distill some of the results of that work. It is a personal document, reflecting the views of the author, and is included in the Bank's publication program to encourage diversity of points of view and discussion.

The objective of meeting basic needs brings to a development strategy a heightened concern with the satisfaction of some elementary needs of the whole population, especially in education and health. The explicit adoption of this objective helps gear production, investment, income, and employment policies to meet the needs of the poor in a cost-effective manner and within a specific time frame. Basic needs is not primarily a welfare concept; improved education and health can make a major contribution to increased productivity.

Past work has shown how economic growth can be combined with redistribution of income and assets to alleviate poverty. Much of what goes under the label of "basic needs" has been contained in previous work on growth with equity, employment creation, integrated rural development, and redistribution with growth. In particular, the emphasis on making the poor more productive has remained an important component of the basic needs approach. Its distinct contribution consists in deepening the income measure of poverty by adding physical estimates of the particular goods and services required to achieve certain results, such as adequate standards of nutrition, health, shelter, water and sanitation, education, and other essentials.

The basic needs approach therefore represents a stage in the evolution of analysis and policy.

In global terms, the elimination of world poverty seems simple. If resources could be shifted to satisfy the basic needs of poverty groups efficiently, the reallocation of only 2 to 3 percent of world income a year would eradicate poverty by the year 2000. But since three-quarters of the world's poor live in very poor countries, the annual cost of eliminating poverty in these countries would be about 15 percent of their national income. The scope for redistribution, with a given set of institutions, is limited. Nevertheless, a selective and targeted approach, sharply focused on basic needs and supported by the international community, is in principle capable of eradicating some of the worst aspects of poverty fairly quickly. The country and sector studies conducted by the World Bank made important contributions to the formulation of such a program. The country studies in particular provided special insights into the problems of poverty and the dimensions of deprivation in each country. Certain common themes emerged from them.

First, the complex question of whether there is a conflict between basic needs and growth has not been conclusively answered. What appeared clear is that better education, nutrition, and health are beneficial in reducing fertility, raising labor productivity, enhancing people's adaptability and capacity for change, and creating a political environment for stable development.

Second, the more pressing basic needs can be met successfully even at quite low levels of income per head, without sacrificing economic growth. For example, life expectancy of sixty-nine years in Sri Lanka was achieved at an income per head of $200 (1977)[1] and at an annual growth rate of income per head of 2 percent between 1960 and 1977, whereas the comparable rate for six other South Asian countries averaged 1.1 percent.

Third, although the longer-term beneficial effect of meeting basic needs on productivity and growth is well established, the country studies showed that even in the short term there is

1. All dollar figures in this book are in current U.S. dollars, unless otherwise specified.

considerable scope for improving basic needs performance by the better management of resources. Reallocating existing resources will help achieve the objective of meeting basic needs. Additional external assistance can help a country embark on such redeployment.

Fourth, it is evident that the redirection of policies toward meeting basic needs often calls for major changes in the power balance in a society. At the same time, a wide variety of political regimes have succeeded in making these changes: from market-oriented economies such as South Korea, to mixed economies such as Sri Lanka, to centrally planned economies such as China and Cuba, to decentralized socialist economies such as Yugoslavia. These different experiences have several characteristics in common: a fairly equitable distribution of physical assets (particularly land), a decentralized administration and delegation of decisionmaking to the local level, with adequate central support, and appropriate policies. In addition, the role of the household, and particularly of women, is more fully recognized in political systems which have had success in meeting basic needs.

The most important part of the World Bank's basic needs work program was the sector studies, which helped identify several operational policy issues. First, linkages and complementarities among various sectors show that interventions, to be more effective and less costly, often need to be simultaneous on several fronts. Basic education, for example, improves the impact of health services, and better health enables children to benefit from education. The effect of investment in sanitation facilities on health status depends on education in personal hygiene. Similarly, curative medical services are unlikely to be very effective if people are chronically malnourished, use germ-infested water, have no sanitation facilities, and follow poor health practices in their personal lives. Provision of additional food to the malnourished may not produce a significant improvement if people suffer from diseases that prevent them from absorbing the food. In extreme cases, action in one sector without corresponding action in others can be counterproductive, as when water is supplied without drainage and thus attracts germs and insects that spread disease.

Second, reallocation of resources within the private sector (especially with respect to food), within the public sector (for example, from defense to education), and from the private to the public sector is often called for. The important question is frequently not how much public revenue is devoted to health or education, but how it is deployed and for whose benefit. Much can be achieved, therefore, without any additional resources, by a reallocation of existing resources.

Third, the correct phasing of sectoral policies and the establishment of priorities is important in order to maximize the self-reinforcing and cumulative impact of some causal sequences. It was found that basic education was essential for meeting other basic needs. Nutrition and health programs can be wasted unless people first adopt practices that render them effective.

Fourth, the sector studies underlined the enormous difficulty of reaching the lowest 20 percent of income earners in a society. Most delivery systems do not reach these people because of existing power structures, market imperfections, or cost considerations. The case for subsidizing certain poverty groups was strengthened by the studies, though many prevailing techniques were found to be inefficient and indiscriminate.

Fifth, all sector studies emphasized the need for providing adequate finance for recurrent costs, which often constitute two-thirds of the total costs of these projects and sectors.

Sixth, particularly severe problems arise in a society in the transition from a more conventional strategy to a basic needs approach, because the production structure is not adapted to the new demand structure. Prices of necessities, especially food, will tend to rise, shortages may emerge, imports will increase, unemployment may arise in the luxury goods sector, and political and administrative difficulties may be added. The international community can play a particularly important role in assisting governments in making this transition and cushioning the economy against some of the disruptions.

These conclusions leave several fundamental issues unresolved. To what extent should meeting basic needs replace the principle of self-help as a guide to international action? To achieve this objective, will it not be necessary to establish enforceable standards of performance to ensure that the benefits actually reach the poverty groups? The new emphasis on basic needs does not resolve these old dilemmas in the field of international economic cooperation. It may even accentuate them.

1

Why Basic Needs?

THE IDEA THAT THE BASIC NEEDS of all should be satisfied before the less essential needs of a few are met is in principle very widely accepted. It goes back to the founders of the world's great religions. More recently, thinkers and practitioners from many countries, international agencies, and bilateral aid donors have made meeting basic human needs a primary objective of development, and it has been embedded in many development plans. Recent discussions were stimulated by the nearly unanimous adoption of a recommendation for a basic needs strategy by the World Employment Conference of the International Labour Organisation (ILO) in 1976.[1]

While there is virtually universal agreement on the objective, there is much disagreement on its precise interpretation and on the most effective way of achieving it. To understand both the wide appeal of the goal and some of the controversies over how to reach it, it is helpful to reflect on the internal logic of the development of the concept and on the way in which accumulating experience has called for successive responses. It is no more, but also no less, than a stage in thinking about and responding to the challenges of development over the past twenty to twenty-five years.[2] If, in the following simplified presentation of the evolution of this thinking, the deficiencies of earlier approaches

1. ILO, *Employment, Growth and Basic Needs: A One-World Problem* (Geneva, 1976).
2. A good survey, to which I am indebted, is to be found in H. W. Singer, "Poverty, Income Distribution and Levels of Living: Thirty Years of Changing Thought on Development Problems," in *Reflections on Economic Development and Social Change: Essays in Honour of Professor V. K. R. V. Rao,* C. H. Hanumantha Rao and P. C. Joshi, eds. (Bombay: Allied Publishers Private Ltd.; Delhi: Institute of Economic Growth, 1979).

and the virtues of the basic needs approach are stressed, this is done to sharpen the distinctive features of basic needs. It does not imply that the previous approaches have not taught us much that is still valuable, or that the basic needs approach is not subject to some of the objections raised to the earlier approaches.

The basic needs strategy is concerned with removing mass deprivation, a concern that has always been at the heart of development. The discussion started in the 1950s, strongly influenced by Sir Arthur Lewis[3] and others, who emphasized economic growth as the way to eradicate poverty. At this early stage, sensible economists and planners were quite clear (in spite of what is now often said in a caricature of past thinking) that growth is not an end in itself, but a performance test of development.

There were three justifications for the emphasis on growth as the principal performance test. One justification assumed that through market forces—such as the rising demand for labor, higher productivity, higher wages, or lower prices—economic growth would spread its benefits widely and speedily, and that these benefits could best be achieved through growth. Of course, even in the early days some skeptics said that growth is not necessarily of this kind. They maintained that in certain conditions (such as increasing returns, restrictions to entry, or unequal distribution of income and assets), growth gives to those who already have; it tends to concentrate income and wealth. Alternatively, it was assumed that governments are democratic, or at any rate are concerned with the fate of the poor. Therefore, progressive taxation, social services, and other government action would spread the benefits downward. The alleviation of poverty would not be automatic, but governments would take action to correct situations in which market forces concentrated benefits. The third justification, more hardheaded than the previous two, said that the fate of the poor should not be a concern in the early stages of development. It was thought necessary first to build up the capital, infrastructure, and productive capacity of an economy so that it could improve the lot of the poor later. For a

3. W. A. Lewis, *The Theory of Economic Growth* (London: Allen and Unwin, 1955).

time—and it could be quite a long period—the poor would have to tighten their belts and the rich would receive most of the benefits. But if the rewards of the rich were used to provide incentives to innovate, to save, and to accumulate capital which could eventually be used to benefit the poor, the early poverty would turn out to have been justified. Some radical egalitarian philosophers such as John Rawls would sometimes sanction such a strategy.[4] Inequalities, in their view, are justified if they are a necessary condition for improving the lot of the poor.

Another strong influence was the so-called Kuznets curve,[5] which relates average income levels to an index of equality and suggests that the early stages of growth are accompanied by growing inequality. Only at an income of about $1,000 per head (1979 dollars) is further growth associated with reduced inequality, measured by the share of the poorest 40 percent of the population. This association has been suggested by tracing the course of the same country over time and of different countries with different incomes at the same time.[6] In the early stages of development, as income per head increases, inequality tends to grow, and this may mean that absolute poverty for some groups also increases. But eventually the turning point, the bottom of the U curve, is reached, after which growing income is accompanied by greater equality and, of course, reduced poverty.

None of the assumptions underlying these three justifications turned out to be universally true. Except for a very few countries, with special initial conditions and policies, there was no automatic tendency for income to be widely spread. Nor did governments always take corrective action to reduce poverty; after all, governments were themselves often formed by people who had close psychological, social, economic, and political

4. John Rawls, *The Theory of Justice* (Cambridge, Mass.: Harvard University Press, 1971), p. 302.

5. Simon Kuznets, "Economic Growth and Income Inequality," *American Economic Review*, vol. 45, no. 1 (March 1955), pp. 1-28; and "Quantitative Aspects of Economic Growth of Nations, VIII: Distribution of Income by Size," *Economic Development and Cultural Change*, vol. 11, no. 2, pt. 2 (January 1963), pp. 1-80.

6. Some people have misinterpreted the Kuznets curve as a kind of iron law of initial inequality, against which policy is powerless. In fact, some countries lie above it, others below.

links with the beneficiaries of the concentrated growth process, even though their motives were often mixed. And it certainly was not the case that a period of enduring mass poverty was needed to accumulate capital. It was found that small-scale farmers saved at least as high a proportion of their income as the big landowners and were more productive, in terms of yield per acre, and that entrepreneurial talent was widespread and not confined to large firms. Prolonged mass poverty was therefore not needed to accumulate savings and capital and to stimulate entrepreneurship.

To judge by the growth of the gross national product (GNP), the development process since World War II has been a spectacular, unprecedented, and unexpected success. Between 1950 and 1975 the income per head in the developing countries, excluding China, grew by 3 percent a year (including China, by 3.4 percent). In West Asia it grew by 5.2, in East Asia by 3.9, in Latin America by 2.6, in Africa by 2.4, and in South Asia by 1.7 percent a year. But at the same time there was increasing dualism. Despite high rates of growth of industrial production and continued general economic growth, not enough employment was created for the rapidly growing labor force. Nor were the benefits of growth always widely spread to the lower income groups.

Arthur Lewis had predicted that subsistence farmers and landless laborers would move from the countryside to the higher-income, urban, modern industries.[7] This move would increase inequality in the early stages (as long as rural inequalities were not substantially greater than urban inequalities), but when more than a critical number of rural poor had been absorbed in modern industry, the golden age would be ushered in, when growth is married to greater equality. It became evident, however, that the Lewis model, which strongly dominated not only academic thought but also political action, did not always work. It did not work for four reasons. (1) The rural-urban income differentials were much higher than had been assumed, owing to trade union

7. W. A. Lewis, "Economic Development with Unlimited Supplies of Labour," *Manchester School of Economic and Social Studies,* vol. 22, no. 2 (May 1954), pp. 139-91.

action on wages, minimum wage legislation, differentials inherited from colonial days, and other causes. This produced an excess of migrants and, at the same time, impeded the rapid absorption of the rural labor force. (2) The rate of growth of the population and the rate of growth of the labor force were much larger than expected. (3) The technology transferred from the rich countries to the urban industrial sector was labor-saving, and though it raised labor productivity it did not create many jobs. (4) In many developing countries a productivity-raising revolution in agriculture was a precondition for substantial and widespread progress in industry, and this revolution did not occur.

It was not surprising, then, that attention turned away from GNP and its growth. Some even called for "dethroning GNP." Since 1969 the International Labour Organisation has attempted to promote jobs. It has organized employment missions to several countries—Colombia, Kenya, the Philippines, Iran, Sri Lanka, the Dominican Republic, the Sudan, and Egypt—to explore ways of creating more jobs. While this was a useful learning exercise, it soon became evident that unemployment is not really the main problem. In *Asian Drama* Gunnar Myrdal devoted many pages to criticizing the concepts of employment, unemployment, and underemployment in the context of underdeveloped Asia.[8] Employment and unemployment make sense only in an industrialized society where there are employment exchanges, organized and informed labor markets, and social security benefits for the unemployed who are trained workers, willing and able to work, but temporarily without a job. Much of this does not apply to the poorest developing countries, in which livelihoods are more important than wage employment. It is an instance of the transfer of an inappropriate intellectual technology from modern societies to the entirely different social and economic conditions of developing countries.

Myrdal talked about "labor utilization," which has numerous dimensions when applied to self-employed subsistence farmers, landless laborers, artisans, traders, educated young people, or

---

8. Gunnar Myrdal, *Asian Drama: An Inquiry into the Poverty of Nations* (New York: Twentieth Century Fund, 1968).

women, in societies without organized labor markets. "Employment" as interpreted in industrial countries is not the appropriate concept. The ILO employment missio.s discovered or rediscovered this, and they also discovered that, to afford to be unemployed, a worker has to be fairly well off. To survive, an unemployed person must have an income from another source. The root problem is poverty, or low-productivity employment, not unemployment. Indeed, the very poor are not unemployed but work very hard and long hours in unremunerative, unproductive forms of activity. This discovery drew attention to the informal sector in the towns: the street traders, garbage collectors, and casual workers, as well as many in small-scale production such as blacksmiths, carpenters, sandal makers, builders, and lamp makers. These people often work extremely hard, are self-employed or employed by their family, and are very poor. Attention was also directed to the women who, in some cultures, perform hard tasks without being counted as members of the labor force because their production is not sold for cash. The problem then was redefined as that of the "working poor."

Labor utilization covers more dimensions than the demand for labor (the lack of which gives rise to Keynesian unemployment) and the need for cooperating factors of production such as machinery and raw materials (the lack of which may be called Marxian "nonemployment"). There is a good deal of evidence that not only labor but also capital is grossly underutilized in many developing countries, which suggests other causes than surplus labor in relation to scarce capital. More specifically, the causes of low labor utilization can be classified under three headings: consumption and level of living, attitudes, and institutions.

Nutrition, health, and education are elements of the level of living that are important for fuller labor utilization. They have been neglected because in rich societies they count as consumption that has no effect on human productivity (though possibly a negative one, as do four-martini lunches). The only exception that is admitted in the literature is some forms of education. In poor countries, however, better nutrition, health, and education can be very productive in developing human resources. (This is one thread that goes into the fabric of basic needs; others are discussed later in this chapter.)

Attitudes make a difference in the kinds of jobs people will accept. In Sri Lanka a large part of unemployment is the result of the high aspirations of the educated, who are no longer prepared to accept "dirty" manual jobs. Caste attitudes in India also present obstacles to fuller labor utilization. In Africa those with primary education wish to leave the land and become clerks in government offices. In many societies manual work or rural work is held in contempt.

The third dimension is the absence or weakness of such institutions as labor exchanges, credit facilities, or an appropriate system of land ownership or tenancy. As a result, labor is underutilized.

For reasons such as these, the concepts of unemployment and underemployment as understood in the North are not applicable, and an approach to poverty that assumes levels of living, attitudes, and institutions adapted to full labor utilization has turned out to be largely a dead end. Unemployment can coexist with considerable labor shortages and capital underutilization.

Inappropriate attitudes and institutions can also frustrate some approaches to meeting basic needs. But focusing on the needs of men, women, and children draws attention to the appropriate institutions (such as public services and credit facilities) to which households need access, and to the attitudes (such as those toward women) that need changing to secure better distribution within the household. These issues will be discussed in greater detail below.

The employment concept was questioned for other reasons too. The creation of more employment opportunities, far from reducing unemployment, increases it. Those who come from the countryside to the towns balance the expectation of high earnings against the probability of getting a job.[9] As job opportunities increase, they attract more people. The influx of migrants in turn contributes to the high rate of urban drift and the growth of shanty towns. The employed urban workers, though poor by

9. John R. Harris and Michael P. Todaro, "Migration, Unemployment, and Development: A Two-Sector Analysis," *American Economic Review,* vol. 60, no. 1 (March 1970), pp. 126–42.

Western standards, are among the better-off when measured against the distribution of income in their own countries.

These difficulties turned the development debate to the question of income distribution. One of the landmarks was the book published in 1974 for the Development Research Center of the World Bank and the Sussex Institute of Development Studies, entitled *Redistribution with Growth*.[10] Among many questions about the relations between growth and distribution[11] it raised two sets of interest in the present context: (1) What can be done to increase the productivity of the small-scale, labor-intensive, informal sector "discovered" by some of the ILO employment missions? How can we remove discrimination against this sector and improve its access to credit, information, and markets? The question is, how does redistribution affect efficiency and growth? Does helping the "working poor" mean sacrificing productivity; is it an efficient way of promoting growth? (2) To turn the question the other way around, how does economic growth affect distribution? It was quite clearly seen that in poor countries growth is a necessary condition for eradicating poverty, but it also seemed that economic growth sometimes reinforced and entrenched inequalities in the distribution of income, assets, and power. Not surprisingly, when growth began with an unequal distribution of assets and power it was more difficult to redistribute income and to eradicate poverty.

Although it was recognized that under these conditions it would be difficult to redistribute existing assets, it was thought that the redistribution of increments of income would be politically easier. (It will be seen that this approach is an elaboration of the second justification for the emphasis on growth mentioned above.) A proportion of incremental income would be taxed and channeled into public services intended to raise the productivity

10. Hollis Chenery and others, *Redistribution with Growth* (London: Oxford University Press, 1974).

11. These questions include: Do conventional measures of growth involve a bias against the poor, and how can this be changed? How can strategies of redistribution be combined with strategies of growth? Is it possible to identify groups whose members have common characteristics and to direct strategies toward those groups? What are the principal instruments of policy?

of the poor. This is "redistribution with growth." But it was discovered that the results of such redistribution are very modest, at any rate for low-income countries. Accu.ding to one simulation exercise, an annual transfer of 2 percent of GNP over twenty-five years into public investment to build up the stock of capital available to the poor—held to be a very "dynamic" policy—would, after forty years, raise the consumption of the poorest 40 percent of the population by only 23 percent; that is to say, their rate of consumption growth would accelerate by 0.5 percent a year: $1 for a $200 income.[12] The model excludes, however, the human capital aspects of some forms of consumption and the impact on labor utilization, which are stressed by the basic needs approach.

In spite of its title, most of *Redistribution with Growth* is concerned not with relative income shares but with the level and growth of income in low-income groups. Much of the redistribution literature measures inequality by the Gini coefficient, which runs through the whole range from the richest to the poorest. It measures somewhat meaningless percentiles instead of socially, regionally, or ethnically significant, deprived groups. It does not tell who is in these decile groups, for how long, or for what reasons. Nor does it indicate the scope for mobility or the degree of equality of opportunity. Of interest to most people is either redistribution from rich to poor or, even more, the reduction of absolute poverty. Normally there is no particular interest in redistribution to the middle, which would reduce inequality but leave poverty untouched. Nor is the fate of income deciles as such of much interest, for these are not sociologically, politically, or humanly interesting groups.

An empirical question is how economic growth affects the reduction of inequality and poverty, and how these reductions in turn affect efficiency and economic growth. The answers to these questions will depend upon the initial distribution of assets, the policies pursued by the government, the available technologies, the scope for labor-intensive exports, which enlarges the

---

12. Chenery and others, *Redistribution with Growth*.

application of labor-intensive technologies, and the rate of population growth. Another empirical question is how policies to reduce inequality and meet basic needs affect freedom. Of concern here are not these empirical questions, nor whether basic needs can be met without reducing inequality, but which objective is more important: reduction in inequality or meeting basic needs; egalitarianism or humanitarianism.

In societies with very low levels of living (and, Wilfred Beckerman argues, in Britain too) meeting basic needs is more important than reducing inequality for three reasons.[13] First, equality as such is probably not an objective of great importance to most people other than utilitarian philosophers and ideologues. Second, this lack of concern is justified, because meeting basic human needs is morally a more important objective than reducing inequality. Third, reducing inequality is a highly complex, abstract objective, open to many different interpretations and therefore operationally ambiguous.

It has been argued that because no group ever asks to be paid *less* in the interest of social justice, people are not really concerned with equality as such.[14] It could be said against this that in democracies people *do* vote for progressive taxes, and a lack of clamor to be paid less may have something to do with the fear that the benefits might go to the fat cats rather than to the underdogs. Nevertheless, most people so rarely perceive they are overpaid that equality as such does not seem to figure prominently in their objectives. And it is fairly plain that many claims for greater social justice are only thinly disguised claims for getting more for oneself.

Removing malnutrition in children, eradicating disease, or educating girls are concrete, specific achievements that meet the basic human needs of deprived groups, whereas reducing inequality is abstract. There is, of course, nothing wrong with an abstract moral objective, but if policies are judged by the evident

---

13. The following discussion owes much to Beckerman's presidential address to the British Association for the Advancement of Science in *Slow Growth in Britain: Causes and Consequences,* Wilfred Beckerman, ed. (Oxford: Clarendon Press, 1979), pp. 9-22.
14. Ibid., p. 11.

reduction of suffering, meeting basic needs scores better than reducing inequality. Internationally, also, there is more concern with ameliorating blatant deprivation than with bringing developing countries up to Western living standards.

It is true that there is no production function for meeting adequate standards of nutrition, health, and education. It is not known precisely which financial, fiscal, and human resources and policies produce these desirable results. The causes are multiple and interact in a complex and still partly unknown manner. But at least it is fairly clear when the objective has been attained, and the criteria by which it is judged are also clear.

In the case of equality, however, no one knows how to achieve (and maintain) it, how precisely to define it, or by what criteria to judge it. To have no clear-cut criteria for defining the optimal degree of equality does not imply ignorance of whether inequality is too great or too small.[15] We may be able to judge improvements in distribution without a clear idea of the optimal distribution, as we may judge whether water in a well is higher or lower without knowing its depth. But the uncertainties surrounding differences in income and assets that are acceptable because of differences in age, sex, location, needs, merit, and so on, and the question of how to resolve conflicts between, for example, merit and need, make it difficult to give precise operational meaning to the objective of redistributive policies: they make "equality" conceptually elusive. A rule is regarded as inegalitarian by Aristotle when equals are awarded unequal shares or unequals are awarded equal shares.[16] But what then defines "equality"? As Robert Nozick has written, "to fill in the blank in 'to each according to his _____' " has been the concern of theories of distributive justice.[17]

It might be objected that poverty necessarily contains a relative component, that it is measured against a standard set by the norms of a society, and that it is therefore closely related to inequality. "Poverty is a relative concept. Saying who is in

15. But see Beckerman (ibid., p. 15).
16. Aristotle, *The Nicomachean Ethics*, bk. 5, 113a, ch. 3 (London and New York: Everyman's Library, 1911), p. 107.
17. Robert Nozick, *Anarchy, State, and Utopia* (New York: Basic Books, 1974), p. 159.

poverty is to make a relative statement rather like saying who is short or heavy."[18] Without rejecting this view, it must be asserted that an irreducible core of absolute deprivation can be determined by medical and physiological criteria, without recourse to reference groups, averages, or other criteria of comparison. In addition to this core of absolute poverty, it has been recognized at least since Adam Smith[19] and Karl Marx[20] that poverty contains a relative component. Whatever doctors, nutritionists, and other scientists may say about the objective conditions of deprivation, how the poor themselves perceive their deprivation is also relevant. This perception is a function of the reference group from which the poor take their standards of what comprises the necessities for a decent minimum level of living. Such a view need not be based on envy. The poverty norm moves up with average income because the desire to belong is an almost biological basic need and is expressed as a desire to live at a standard that is regarded by the society as decent. This standard will be different in the United States from what it is in Sri Lanka (see table 1).[21] But it may be questioned whether

18. Brian Abel-Smith and Peter Townsend, *The Poor and the Poorest* (London: G. Bell and Sons, 1965), p. 63. Peter Townsend defines poverty as "the absence of inadequacy of those diets, amenities, standards, services, and activities which are common or customary in society. People are deprived of the conditions of life which ordinarily define membership of society. If they lack or are denied resources to obtain access to these conditions of life, and so fulfil membership of society, they are in poverty." (*Poverty in the United Kingdom: A Survey of Household Resources and Standards of Living* [Berkeley and Los Angeles: University of California Press, 1979], p. 915.) This leads to the paradoxical conclusion that there is no poverty in societies where nearly everybody lives in conditions of deprivation which "ordinarily define membership of society."

19. "By necessities I understand not only the commodities which are indispensably necessary for the support of life, but whatever the custom of the country renders it indecent for creditable people, even of the lowest order, to be without." (Adam Smith, *The Wealth of Nations*, bk. 5, ch. 2, pt. 2.)

20. "A house may be large or small: as long as the surrounding houses are equally small it satisfies all social demands for a dwelling. But let a palace arise beside the little house, and it shrinks from a little house to a hut . . . however high it [the little house] may shoot up in the course of civilization, if the neighboring palace grows to an equal or even greater extent, the occupant of the relatively small house will feel more and more uncomfortable, dissatisfied and cramped within its four walls." (Karl Marx and Frederick Engels, *Selected Works*, vol. 1 [Moscow: Foreign Languages Publishing House, 1958], pp. 93-94.)

21. Table 1 illustrates the wide differences among poverty lines for countries at different income levels. The more than thirtyfold difference between the lowest and the

(*Note continues on p. 20.*)

Table 1. *Gross Domestic Product per Head
and Poverty Norm (Excluding Rent)
in Selected Countries for Selected Years*

Country	Year	GDP per head (U.S. dollars)	Single person poverty norm (percentage of GDP per head)
United States	1965	3,240	25.8 [a]
Switzerland	1966	2,265	30.3
Canada	1965	2,156	23.3 [b]
Denmark	1965	2,070	24.4
Finland	1967	1,801	24.1
France	1965	1,626	22.4
United Kingdom	1963	1,395	32.8
West Germany	1962	1,321	25.4
Japan	1964	717	30.3
Ireland	1962	639	24.3
Singapore	1958	435	14.0
Hong Kong	1958	257	6.1
Ceylon	1963	136	18.5
Egypt	1953	92	21.0

a. The general assistance standard of Santa Clara County, Calif.
b. The general assistance standard of the Province of Ontario.
Source: Koji Taira, "Consumer Preferences, Poverty Norms and Extent of Poverty,"
Quarterly Review of Economics and Business, vol. 9, no. 2 (July 1969), table 1, p. 37.

poverty should be defined in such a way that it can never be
reduced, however much absolute income levels rise, if the measure of inequality remains unchanged. This would make poverty
eradication rather like the electric hare used to spur on
greyhounds at dog races.[22] It is, however, an empirical fact that

---

highest incomes in the table would be reduced if purchasing power instead of exchange
rates were used for conversion, but a substantial difference would remain.
    22. A. K. Sen concluded his discussion of relative deprivation: "It is, however, worth
noting that the approach of relative deprivation—even including all its variants—cannot
really be the only basis for the concept of poverty. There is an irreducible core of *absolute*
deprivation in our idea of poverty which translates reports of starvation, malnutrition and
visible hardship into a diagnosis of poverty without having to ascertain first the relative
picture. The approach of relative deprivation supplements rather than competes with this
concern with absolute dispossession." (*Three Notes on the Concept of Poverty,* World
Employment Programme Research Working Paper, WEP2-23/WP65 (Geneva: ILO,
1978), p. 11.

the only societies that have been successful in meeting basic needs are those that have also reduced inequalities.

After the dead end of "employment" as interpreted in industrial countries and the limitation and irrelevance of egalitarianism, basic human needs is the next logical step in the path of development thinking. Zooming in on basic needs has at least four fundamental advantages over previous approaches to growth, employment, income redistribution, and poverty eradication.

First, and most important, the basic needs concept is a reminder that the objective of the development effort is to provide all human beings with the *opportunity* for a full life. However a "full life" is interpreted, the opportunity for achieving it presupposes meeting basic needs. In the past two decades, those concerned with development have sometimes got lost in the intricacies of means—production, productivity, savings ratios, export ratios, capital-output ratios, tax ratios, and so on—and lost sight of the end. They came near to being guilty, to borrow a term from Marx, of "commodity fetishism." Being clear about the end obviously does not mean neglecting the means: on the contrary, it means efforts are directed to choosing the right means for the ultimate ends that are desired. In the past, planners have moved away from one aim of development, which is meeting basic human needs, to some conglomeration of commodities and services valued at market prices, irrespective of whether they are air conditioners or bicycles, luxury houses or rural shelters, whether they benefit the rich or the poor. The basic needs approach recalls the fundamental concern of development, which is human beings and their needs.

Second, the approach goes beyond abstractions such as money, income, or employment. These aggregates have their place and function; they are important concepts and should not be abandoned; but they are useless if they conceal the specific, concrete objectives that are sought. To consider basic needs is to move from the abstract to the concrete, from the aggregate to the specific.

The evolution sketched above shows that the concepts have become decreasingly abstract and increasingly disaggregated, concrete, and specific. Starting with GNP and its growth, a highly abstract and unspecified conglomerate of goods and services, irrespective of what and for whom, development thinking then turned to employment, a somewhat more specific goal. The discussion was increasingly narrowed down to particular groups of unemployed: school leavers, recent migrants to the city, landless laborers, small-scale farmers without water supply, and so forth. But "employment" also was seen to have serious limitations. Ideas were further narrowed to identify deprived groups of individuals and families—women, children under five, the elderly, youths with specific needs, ethnic groups discriminated against, communities in distant and neglected regions.

Third, the basic needs approach appeals to members of the national and international community and is therefore capable of mobilizing resources, unlike vaguer (though important) objectives, such as raising growth rates to 6 percent, contributing 0.7 percent of GNP to development assistance, redistributing for greater equality, or narrowing income gaps. People do not normally share lottery prizes or other gains in wealth with their grown brothers and sisters, but they do help when their siblings are ill, or their children need education, or some other basic need has to be met. The same is true in the wider human family.[23] Meeting basic needs has something of the nature of a public good. My satisfaction from knowing that a hungry child is fed does not detract from someone else's satisfaction. The basic needs approach therefore has the power to mobilize support for policies that more abstract notions lack.

Fourth, the approach has great organizing and integrating power intellectually, as well as politically. It provides a key to the solution of problems that are apparently separate, but, on inspection, prove to be related. If basic needs is made the starting point, these otherwise recalcitrant problems fall into place and become solvable.

In one sense, this is a homecoming. For when the world embarked on development thirty years ago, it was primarily

23. Arnold C. Harberger, "On the Use of Distributional Weights in Social Cost-Benefit Analysis," *Journal of Political Economy*, vol. 86, no. 2, pt. 2 (April 1978), supplement, pp. S87–S120.

with the needs of the poor in mind. Third World leaders wanted economic as well as political independence, but independence was to be used for man's self-fulfillment. The process got side-tracked, but many important things were discovered about development: the importance of making small-scale farmers and members of the informal urban sector more productive and raising their earning power; the scope for "efficient" redistribution, that is, redistribution that contributes to a more equitable economic growth; the numerous dimensions of labor markets; and the importance of creating demand for certain types of product and the labor producing them.

As early as the 1950s pioneers such as Pitambar Pant[24] in India and Lauchlin Currie, who led the first World Bank mission to a developing country (Colombia), said that development must be concerned with meeting minimum or basic human needs (though their strategies were strongly growth-oriented). Now there is a deeper understanding of the issues, of many of the inhibitions, obstacles, and constraints, and also a clearer vision of the path.

Basic Needs as an Integrating Concept

One merit of the basic needs concept is that it provides a powerful basis for organizing analysis and policymaking. Just as it can mobilize political support, it is also capable of integrating thought and action in different fields. This could be illustrated in the areas of energy, environmental pollution, raw material exhaustion, appropriate technology, appropriate consumption patterns, urbanization, rural-urban migration, international

24. Pitambar Pant, "Perspective of Development, India 1960–61 to 1975–76: Implications of Planning for a Minimum Level of Living," in *Poverty and Income Distribution in India*, T. N. Srinivasan and P. K. Bardhan, eds. (Calcutta: Statistical Publishing Society, 1974). In a paper that was circulated in August 1962 by the Perspective Planning Division of the Planning Commission, part of which is reprinted in the above book, Pitambar Pant anticipated many features of the basic needs approach. But, since he believed with Pareto in the similarity of income distributions in all societies, minimum needs had to be met by general economic growth. He postulated this growth to be much higher than the five-year-plan target, which, in turn, was higher than actual growth. Moreover, he regarded the poorest 20 percent as unreachable by economic growth.

trade, dominance and dependence, and the treatment of transnational corporations. A host of technical and apparently disparate problems are seen to be connected and become amenable to
solution once it is assumed that the ultimate purpose of development is to meet the basic needs of individuals.

For example, much of the criticism of inefficient, high-cost
industrialization behind high walls of protection should be
directed not at industrialization as such, but at the products and
techniques that cater to a small privileged group and reflect
entrenched vested interests. Industrialization that is geared to the
needs of the mass of the people has different implications for
choice of product, choice of technology, foreign trade, and
investment[25]

A development strategy guided by the goal of meeting the
basic needs of the poor points to a different composition of
products and choice of techniques. A strategy to make income
distribution more egalitarian is likely to encourage more labor-
intensive methods of production and thereby generate jobs and
primary sources of income for the poor. It also is likely to reduce
the demand that rapid urbanization makes on scarce capital,
scarce skills, and exhaustible natural resources. By raising the
level of living of the poor in the countryside, such a strategy
reduces the pressure to leave the farmsteads and to expand expensive services in the large cities. By redirecting the composition of production toward products consumed by the poor, it
encourages more intra–Third World trade, so that developing
countries produce more of what they consume, and consume
more of what they produce.

This does not mean that opting for a basic needs style of
development is easy. The required changes in power relations
and in the direction of research and development, the more
complex system of decentralized administration, and the needed
coordination of trade and investment policy with negotiations
with transnationals are clearly enormously difficult tasks. The
point, however, is that no progress is possible unless the fundamental objective is borne in mind.

25. For an elaboration, see Paul Streeten, "Industrialization in a Unified Development
Strategy," *World Development,* vol. 3, no. 1 (January 1975), pp. 1-9.

The international community can support efforts at reorientation toward basic needs. As it happens, for quite different historical reasons, the specialized agencies of the United Nations are already organized to meet the principal basic needs: WHO for health, Unesco for basic education, FAO for food and agriculture, ILO for employment, UNICEF for children and their families. Their efforts are not now always concentrated on meeting human needs, and they often lack the coordination that would be needed for a concerted attack on the problem of poverty. But the challenge is there, and the institutional framework for the response exists.

Interpretations

Interpretations of the basic needs approach have proliferated since 1976. It may therefore be helpful to list briefly the main interpretations of the concept and to classify them according to specific goals, political implications, and methods of implementation. Such a classification will reduce misunderstandings by making it clear which concept each protagonist in a debate is talking about.

What Are Basic Needs and Who Determines Them?

Basic needs may be interpreted in terms of minimum specified quantities of such things as food, clothing, shelter, water, and sanitation that are necessary to prevent ill health, undernourishment, and the like. This narrow, physiological interpretation has the strongest moral appeal, but it leaves open many questions, such as the precise relation between food intake and adequate nutrition, and the most effective way of providing the resources to satisfy needs.

Basic needs may be interpreted subjectively as the satisfaction of consumers' wants as perceived by the consumers themselves, rather than by physiologists, doctors, and other specialists. This interpretation leads to the conclusion that people should be given opportunities to earn the incomes necessary to purchase the basic goods and services. This interpretation is the most natural approach for neoclassical economists, who assume that consumers are better judges of their basic needs than experts, but it leaves open the demarcation of the domain of the public sector—and of policy interventions.

Those who reject the assumption that consumers are rational (that is, that they have full access to information, are able and ready to act on it, and are not subject to pressures, enticements, cajolery, irrational fears, and so on) arrive at a more interventionist interpretation. According to this view, public authorities not only decide the design of public services such as water supply, sanitation, and education, but also guide private consumption in the light of public considerations (for example, through counterpressures to advertisers or food subsidies). Those hostile to this interpretation call it paternalistic; those sympathetic to it call it discriminating or selective or educational.

A fourth interpretation emphasizes the noneconomic, nonmaterial aspects of human autonomy and embraces individual and group participation in the formulation and implementation of projects, and in some cases political mobilization. This widely ranging sociopolitical interpretation sometimes verges on the notion that the satisfaction of basic needs is a human right: freedom from want is like the right not to be tortured. In its more general formulation it comes near the view that "all good things go together." In its narrower formulation nonmaterial needs are seen as ends, separate from the material means for the satisfaction of what are sometimes called material needs.

What Are the Political Criteria?

According to one interpretation, the basic needs approach is revolutionary because it calls for the radical redistribution not only of income and assets but also of power, and for the political mobilization of the poor themselves. This interpretation draws on the experience of China.

At the other extreme, the approach has been interpreted as a minimum welfare sop to keep the poor quiet. The emphasis on rural development, self-help, and local resources has generated the fear that industrialized countries will use basic needs as a "cop-out" from international commitments. According to this most conservative interpretation, the intention of the basic needs approach is to keep reactionary regimes in power and to prevent the radical reforms that industrialization or egalitarianism requires.

An intermediate interpretation is that basic needs have been met by a variety of political regimes (North and South Korea, China and the authorities on Taiwan, Costa Rica and Cuba), and that a revolution is neither a necessary nor a sufficient condition (revolutions have gone wrong). It is clear that some political regimes are incapable of meeting basic needs, but basic needs are not the monopoly of one creed.

What Are the Methods of Implementation?

One method of implementation consists of counting the number of the deprived, figuring the cost of the goods and services needed to eradicate deprivation, and delivering them to the "target groups." This has been called the "count, cost, and deliver" approach. There are capital and recurrent costs, local and foreign costs, and inputs such as labor, capital, and land. A social accounting matrix can be used to derive employment and income distribution from the structure of production.

Another interpretation insists on the need to provide earning opportunities for the poor, to raise their productivity, and to improve their access to both inputs and markets. But this leaves out the unemployables, the old and the young, the disabled, the sick. It also leaves out intrahousehold distribution.

A third interpretation emphasizes the organizational and institutional requirements of meeting basic needs. It examines the relation between central and local decisionmaking, the institutions needed to mediate between demand and supply, and the organizational requirements of supply management.

A fourth interpretation stresses the need to mobilize the social and political power of the poor and to permit full participation in the design, execution, and monitoring of anti-poverty projects. According to this interpretation, a basic needs approach must avoid focusing on basic needs as such and concentrate instead on the political processes by which the system that perpetuates poverty can be destroyed or reformed.

How Have the Poor Fared?

In the foregoing pages, I discussed the evolution of ideas about and responses to the development process. Ideas and economic facts interact and the question arises: How have the poor in fact fared in the past fifteen to twenty-five years? Before answering it, certain preliminary questions have to be asked, if not answered.

First, how should the poor be identified? The common practice of using deciles (or quintiles or quartiles) of income recipients has serious defects. Should they be identified by social and economic classes? Or by (rural or urban) residence? Or, a somewhat neglected approach, by ethnic groups or by regions? Or by the stage in the age cycle (the very young and old), or by family size and age of head of the family? Or as particular members of families, such as children under five years old and women? Poverty has many dimensions, and concentration on deciles— even if adjusted for relative price changes, post-tax incomes, and social services—may obscure some of these.

Second, is poverty absolute or relative? Poverty lines vary between climates, cultures, and social environments. But is there a component of poverty that has to be defined in relation to the mean income, or to the bottom of the 80 percent above the poorest 20 percent of the population, or to some other measure that is regarded as a minimum decent standard in a society? The need to relate poverty to some acceptable social standard or some reference group is partly psychological, stemming from the need to belong, and is partly related to the nature of economic progress (see below in this section). It has even been questioned whether the distinction between relative and absolute poverty is valid. If it is valid, which should be the main concern? Some answers to these questions were offered earlier in this chapter.

Third, it may be asked whether the absolute number of poor or the proportion of poor in the total population has increased. With rapidly growing populations, it may be thought that the relevant concept for judging the success of strategies in eliminating poverty should be the proportion of poor.

Fourth, how does one proceed from money income shares, which are known but irrelevant, to real income shares or income levels, which are relevant but unknown, in assessing inequality and poverty? Ideally, there should be an index of the minimum-needs cost-of-living that allows for price changes and consequential substitution between items in the basket. It might then be possible to make estimates of what Seebohm Rowntree, many decades ago in his research on poverty in York, called "secondary poverty."[26] This refers to real incomes adequate to buy the minimum-needs basket, with allowance for the fact that people, for a variety of reasons, do not spend their incomes exclusively on minimum needs. General consumer price indexes are not relevant to poverty indexes.

There are four distinct issues. (1) In developing countries, even more than in developed countries, different groups do not face the same prices for the same goods. The urban cost-of-living is higher than the rural, and regional costs vary. For this reason money income shares may overstate inequalities and rural poverty. (2) Different groups consume different goods, and the same goods in different proportions. Prices do not rise proportionately for all groups. Food forms a higher proportion of total expenditure for the poor, and if its price rises by more than average prices, poverty is underestimated by money income shares. The same problem arises for both cross-sectional and time series data. (3) With rising average standards, certain items especially important to the poor may cease to be available and be replaced by more expensive items, and the same items may be subject to more sophisticated treatment through more packaging, higher degrees of processing, or other "improvements"

---

26. B. Seebohm Rowntree, *Poverty: A Study of Town Life* (London: Macmillan, 1901).

which raise the cost to the poor, especially the urban poor or subsistence farmers switching to cash crops. (4) Some items counted as final goods and therefore part of income may be more properly regarded as intermediate goods, such as the journey to work or urban requirements of "proper" dress.

Fifth, is consumption or income the more appropriate measure? Data for consumption and for income are sometimes inconsistent. Consumption is more closely related to "permanent income," where income fluctuates or is subject to change. Consumption may also be thought to be the appropriate welfare concept. There is always an advantage in supplementing income measures by measures of physical volume such as food consumption. There are several layers to penetrate, each of which may give different results. Behind money income there is real income; instead of real income it may be desirable to measure consumption; behind consumption there is nutritious food; behind nutritious food, its characteristics such as caloric and protein content; and behind these are health levels reflected in morbidity and longevity.

Sixth, there is the question of mobility, both in the social and economic scale and by residence. It is, for example, possible for the proportion of the rural poor to increase, without anyone's becoming worse off, simply because some of the rural better-off move to the towns. Similarly, urban poor may increase because the rural poor have moved to towns. It may also be asked whether the members (and families) of the group have largely remained the same or whether the composition has changed. The evaluation and tolerance of poverty will be different according to the length of time members of poverty groups stay in them. Are their expectations of improving their lot the same or do some identifiable groups feel that opportunities are barred?

Seventh, should cross-country regressions or time series be used? Cross-country evidence tends to neglect policy options, but time series data are unreliable and, if general conclusions are drawn from them, may encourage undue determinism. The twentieth century is different from the nineteenth, and its last fifth may turn out to be different from the one before, just as Taiwan is different from Brazil.

Eighth, it might be asked whether it is important to know the facts. We may say Yes because what we know, or think we know, enters into our models and policies. But firm knowledge is very hard to gain. The fate of the English poor during the Industrial Revolution is still an unsettled issue. Action cannot wait for the results of research.

With these preliminary questions in mind, it is possible to return to the main question: how have inequality and absolute poverty changed over the past twenty years? The question of inequality raises, in turn, two others: How is inequality at any given time related to growth, and how are changes in inequality related to growth?

The main lesson is that, although the figures are unreliable, there is no correlation between either point inequality or changes in inequality and rates of growth. A vast variety of experience indicates that there are fast growers with equality (Taiwan in 1964–68 and later South Korea) and fast growers with inequality (Puerto Rico, Colombia, and the Philippines.) There are fast growers that have become more equal (Taiwan in 1959–64 and since 1968, and South Korea in the earlier period, though the evidence for both has been questioned), and there are fast growers that have become less equal (Mexico, Brazil, Peru, and Malaysia). There are slow growers that have been unequal and slow growers that remained unequal (India). Finally, there are slow growers that have become more equal (such as Sri Lanka, though the evidence is controversial) and slow growers that have become less equal (some states in India).

In the light of the previous discussion, the more interesting question is: What has happened to absolute poverty? The data do not permit an answer in terms of the satisfaction of basic needs, though in chapter 5 some experiences will be presented. For the moment, poverty is defined in terms of a poverty line: the level of income that enables all members of the household to be fed adequately.

In South Korea, Taiwan, Hong Kong, Singapore, and China, rapid growth was combined with a substantial reduction in the number of poor people. This group covers 1 billion people, or 35 percent of the population of the Third World. But the figures depend crucially on the high growth rates of China, which are controversial.

In a second group, including the Philippines, Malaysia, Turkey, Argentina, Mexico, and Brazil, rapid or moderate growth was accompanied by growing inequality but not by absolute impoverishment, though also not by spectacular progress of the poor. This group comprises 25 percent of the population of the Third World.

In a third group, including Bangladesh and the poorer African countries, slow growth was accompanied by absolute impoverishment. The evidence on India, Indonesia, and Pakistan is disputed. In India periods of high agricultural growth were accompanied by improvement of the lot of the poor, except in the Punjab, where high growth appears to have left the proportion unchanged. (Some of this may be accounted for by immigration.) Even in these poor countries indicators for the health and education of the poor show improvement, so that on that score the poor are better off. Since this group contains some very large countries and comprises 40 percent of the population of the Third World, it is crucial for any general lessons. Yet the evidence is inconclusive and disputed. There is no doubt there are absolutely more poor, but whether the proportion is larger is less certain.[27]

The Basic Needs Approach

There are two ways of defining a basic needs approach to development. The first sees it as the culmination of twenty-five years of development thought and experience. According to this definition, the basic needs approach embraces the components of previous strategies and approaches, such as rural development, the alleviation of urban poverty, the creation of employment

27. For a fuller treatment of some of these issues, to which this section is indebted, see David Morawetz, *Twenty-five Years of Economic Development, 1950 to 1975* (Baltimore, Md.: Johns Hopkins University Press, 1977); and "Basic Needs Policies and Population Growth," *World Development*, vol. 6, no. 11/12 (November/December 1978), pp. 1251-59.

through small-scale industries, redistribution with growth, and other poverty-, employment-, and equity-oriented approaches, especially those aimed at making the poor more productive. The merit of such a definition is that it rallies a wide variety of people, interests, and institutions under the appealing banner of basic needs. The new elements are a shift toward social services, households, and their linkages to help and mobilize the poor, and an emphasis on so-called new-style projects in nutrition, health, and education. The fact that the basic needs approach means many things to many people is, from this point of view, an advantage.

But there are also drawbacks in elevating the approach to an all-embracing, almost exclusive development strategy. This definition is intellectually clumsy because of the difficulties of demarcation and of incorporating objectives other than basic needs, and it suffers from political unreality. More generally, this definition tends to blur the features that distinguish the basic needs approach from other strategies and makes it more difficult to define areas of disagreement and thereby reach agreement.

The second definition of a basic needs approach brings out sharply its distinctive features and describes it as supplementing or complementing existing strategies. It emphasizes the paradigmatic change. This approach has the tactical defects of its intellectual merits: it tends to evoke controversy, arouse opposition to certain aspects, and may reduce the chances of reaching agreement on action. But it has intellectual and political appeal because it cannot be accused of simply pouring old wine into new bottles or of concealing behind a polemical slogan questions calling for serious analysis and experiment.

In this section, to clarify the basic needs approach, an attempt will be made to define its differentiating features. It then becomes not *a* development strategy but an adjunct to, and a modification of, existing development strategies. In the rest of the book, however, the term will be used in its broader meaning.

A basic needs approach to development attempts to provide the opportunities for the full physical, mental, and social development of the human personality and then derives the ways of achieving this objective. Within a short time, say, one generation, it tries to ensure access to particular resources (such as caloric adequacy) for particular groups (defined by age, sex, or activity) that are deficient in these resources. These groups might be malnourished children under five or rural communities in distant regions where harvests are uncertain; they might be rural women, or ethnic groups that are discriminated against, or the old and infirm. They cannot be captured by deciles in an abstract scale of income distribution. The basic needs approach concentrates on what is provided and its effect on needs such as health rather than on income alone. It does not replace the more aggregate and abstract concepts, which remain essential to measurement, integration, and analysis; it gives them content. Nor does it replace concepts such as productivity, production, and growth, which are means to broader ends; but the end of meeting basic human needs may require changing the composition of output, the rates of growth of its different components, the distribution of purchasing power, the design of social services and taxes, and the distribution system within the household.

In addition to the concrete specification of human needs in contrast (and as a supplement) to abstract concepts, and the emphasis on ends in contrast to means, the basic needs approach encompasses nonmaterial needs. Although the means to their satisfaction cannot be dispensed, as they can for material needs, they are a vital component of a basic needs approach. This can be seen by imagining a situation in which all material needs are met but not the others. A zoo or, worse, a well-run prison delivers the basic needs basket efficiently to the target groups, but basic *human* needs are not met. Nonmaterial needs are important not only because they are valued in their own right, but also because they are important conditions for meeting material needs. They include the needs for self-determination, self-reliance, and security, for the participation of workers and citizens in the decision-making that affects them, for national and cultural identity, and for a sense of purpose in life and work. While some of these nonmaterial needs are conditions for meeting the more material needs, there may be conflict between others. In China, for example, the effective pursuit of basic needs has been in conflict with the civil rights of some groups. For other sets of needs, there may be neither complementarity nor conflict.[28]

Income Approach versus Basic Needs

The income approach recommends measures that raise the real incomes of the poor by making them more productive, so that the purchasing power of their earnings, together with the yield of their subsistence production, enables them to acquire the basic needs basket. There can be no doubt that efforts to make the poor more productive and their activities more remunerative are central to all poverty-oriented development strategies. And some features of the basic needs approach were contained in the earlier approaches. The basic needs approach in the narrow sense, however, regards the income-orientation of earlier approaches as incomplete and partial, for seven reasons.

1. Some basic needs can be satisfied only, or more effectively, through public services (education, health, water, sanitation), through subsidized goods and services, or through transfer payments. These services call for progressive taxation, for indirect taxation of luxury goods, for ensuring that the poor have access to the services, and for a system of checks against abuse. The provision of public services is, of course, not a distinctive feature of the basic needs approach. But the approach is distinguished by its emphasis on investigating why these services have so often failed to reach the groups for whom they were intended, or were claimed to be intended, and why they have often reinforced inequalities in the distribution of private income. By redesigning these services, the basic needs approach ensures that they do reach the poor.

2. There is some evidence that consumers (both poor and rich) are not always efficient, especially in optimizing nutrition and health, and especially in the case of subsistence farmers who become cash earners. Additional cash income is sometimes spent

---

28. It may be thought that the notion "basic" precludes possibilities of conflict and tradeoffs. But, since not all needs can be met at once, the hierarchy is arranged as a succession in time.

on food of lower nutritional value than that previously consumed (as when polished rice is substituted for coarse grains, or
rice for wheat) or on items other than food.

3. The manner in which additional income is earned may
affect nutrition adversely. Female employment may reduce
breast feeding and therefore the nutrition of babies, even though
the mother's income has risen. More profitable cash crops may
replace "inferior" and cheaper crops, such as millets, that are
grown for home use; or dairy farming, though it creates employment, may divert land from cheaper but more nutritious maize.
The human energy costs of producing a cash crop that replaces
subsistence agriculture may be so great in relation to wages that
the dependent members of the family are systematically deprived
of adequate nutrition.[29] In such a situation more food would
mean lower levels of nutrition. Hydroelectric dams and irrigation or drainage schemes, while raising incomes, can contribute
to the spread of water-borne diseases, such as malaria,
onchocerciasis, and schistosomiasis. In some cases, the extra
costs of preventing these diseases are more than offset by the
additional returns from the project. But in other cases, the fate of
the victims has no bearing on the project.

Both reasons 2 and 3 raise difficult and controversial questions
about free choice and society's right to intervene, and about
effective methods of aiding choice and strengthening and
reaching the weak.[30]

4. There is maldistribution within households, as well as between households; women and children tend to have a lower
proportion of their needs met than do males. In many societies
women also carry the heaviest work load, so that it cannot be
argued that food is distributed according to effort.

29. Daniel R. Gross and Barbara A. Underwood, "Technological Change and Caloric
Costs: Sisal Agriculture in Northeastern Brazil, *American Anthropologist,* vol. 73, no. 3
(June 1971), pp. 725-40.

30. It is often regarded as objectionable to maintain that others may know better than
the individuals concerned what is good for them. Even in rich societies, however, people
delegate decisionmaking to their doctors and to the teachers of their children. Every-
where there are numerous exceptions to the textbook principle that the individual knows
best what is in his own interest.

5. A substantial proportion of the destitute are sick, disabled, aged, or orphaned; they may be members of households or they may not. Their needs can be met only through transfer payments or public services since, by definition, they are incapable of earning. This group has been neglected by the income and productivity approach to poverty alleviation and employment creation. Of course, the problems of implementation are particularly difficult. Even some quite affluent societies have not been successful in eradicating the poverty of their handicapped, and societies with very meager resources have a much more difficult task.

6. The income approach has paid a good deal of attention to the choice of technique but has neglected to provide for appropriate products. Many developing societies import or produce domestically oversophisticated products that meet excessive needs transferred from relatively high-income, high-saving economies. This has frustrated the pursuit of a basic needs approach by catering to the demand of a small section of the population or by preempting an excessive slice of the low incomes of the poor. An essential feature of the basic needs approach is to choose appropriate final products and produce them by appropriate techniques, thereby giving rise to more jobs and a more even income distribution, which in turn generates the demand for these products. This goal cannot necessarily be fully achieved by a redistribution of income and reliance on market responses (though foreign trade is not ruled out).

7. As already mentioned, the income approach neglects the importance of nonmaterial needs, both in their own right and as instruments of meeting some material needs more effectively, at lower cost, and in a shorter period. This point becomes particularly relevant if the nonsatisfaction of nonmaterial needs (such as participation) increases the difficulty of meeting basic needs more than that of achieving income growth.

The Case for Basic Needs

The hypothesis of the basic needs approach is that a set of selective policies makes it possible to satisfy the basic human needs of the whole population at levels of income per head substantially below those required by a less discriminating strategy of all-round income growth—and it is therefore possible to satisfy these needs sooner. If a military but apt metaphor is permitted, the choice is between precision bombing and devastation bombing. Attacking the evils of hunger, malnutrition, disease, and illiteracy with precision will eradicate (or at least ameliorate) these evils with fewer resources (or sooner) than would the roundabout method of raising incomes.

Two crucial assumptions must be made: one of value and one of fact. The opposition to the basic needs approach hinges on the rejection of either or both of these assumptions. The value assumption is that substantially less importance is attached to the uses of all extra resources that do not meet basic needs. It may be objected that governments and people who do not accept this value judgment will reject the whole approach, and those that do accept it will not need to be exhorted. But aid agencies might wish to adopt the value judgment, and since governments and people do not have monolithic value systems, they might be induced to accept it by dialogue and selective support.

The crucial factual assumption is that leakages, inefficiencies, and "trickle-up" (which makes the better-off the ultimate beneficiaries of anti-poverty policies) are smaller in a selective system than in a general system. The wastage of the basic needs approach may be as large as, or even larger than, that of the income-oriented, nonselective approach. There is some evidence that this need not be so. But this is an important area for operational research and experimentation. Some fairly firm conclusions that have already emerged from work on sectors and countries are discussed in subsequent chapters.

It is possible to speak of a gap between available resources and resources required to meet basic needs, though this is a somewhat mechanical view because it neglects alternative methods of mobilizing these resources. The great merit of a basic needs approach, however, is that it can close this gap more successfully for two reasons. First, it requires fewer resources to close the gap in a given time, or the same resources can close it more quickly; second, it makes more resources available.

Fewer resources are required, or the objective can be achieved sooner, because a direct attack on deprivation economizes on the resources for which income would otherwise be spent and which do not contribute to meeting basic needs. These include, in addition to improvements in the instruments of implementation, the non-basic needs items in the consumption expenditure of the poor; part of the consumption expenditure of the better-off that is not needed as an incentive for them to manage, innovate, and take risks; and investment expenditure to the extent that its reduction does not detract from constructing the sustainable base for meeting basic needs.[31] In addition, the fewer resources that are needed show a higher "productivity" in meeting basic needs. A combined operation for providing an appropriately selected package of basic needs (water, sewerage, nutrition, and health) economizes on the use of resources and improves the impact because of linkages, complementarities, and interdependencies between different sectors.

A direct attack to reduce infant mortality,[32] to educate women, and—the apparently purest form of welfare—to provide for old age, illness, and disability is thought to reduce the desired family size and fertility rates more speedily and at lower cost than raising household incomes, at any rate after a time lag in which the population growth rate may rise.[33] (Alternatively, the reduction in population growth can be regarded as helping increase available resources.) Freedom from unwanted pregnancies is,

31. To the extent that meeting basic needs covers provision for the victims of disasters (floods, earthquakes, or droughts), special arrangements are required and the argument of the text applies with less force.

32. Very low birth rates are registered in countries (such as Sri Lanka, China, and South Korea) with low infant mortality rates and high life expectancy.

33. Robert H. Cassen, "Population and Development: A Survey," *World Development*, vol. 4, no. 10/11 (October/November 1976), pp. 785-830. Cassen emphasizes the complex processes connecting these "correlates of fertility decline" and other aspects of development, including income and fertility. Morawetz confirms statistically the link between basic needs and fertility decline; see "Basic Needs Policies and Population Growth." For some criticisms of this view, see Nick Eberstadt, "Recent Declines in Fertility in Less Developed Countries," *World Development*, vol. 8, no. 1 (January 1980), pp. 37-60, and the sources quoted there; and Frank L. Mott and Susan Mott, "Kenya's Record Population Growth: A Dilemma of Development," *Population Bulletin*, vol. 55, no. 5 (October 1980), pp. 758-830.

moreover, itself a basic need. If met, it does not reduce the desired family size, but it reduces fertility rates by decreasing the number of unwanted births. In these ways—saving resources otherwise expended on objectives with lower priority than basic needs, economizing on linkages, and reducing fertility rates (and, on certain assumptions about the relation between mortality and fertility rates, reducing population growth)—the basic needs approach economizes on the use of resources and on the time needed to satisfy basic needs.

This approach will also tend to make more resources available, both domestically and (possibly) internationally. More resources will be available domestically for three reasons. First, the composition of output needed to satisfy basic needs is likely to be produced more labor intensively.[34] In countries with underemployed labor, this will raise not only employment but also production. Second, an attack on malnutrition, disease, and illiteracy not only lengthens life and improves its quality (desirable goals in their own right) but also improves the quality of the labor force.[35] It is, however, an open question whether the narrowly interpreted economic returns to this form of human investment are higher, at the margin, than those from more conventional investment in physical capital. Third, a basic needs approach that is based on participation will mobilize local resources in many ways. Paramedical personnel and teachers can be (partly) paid in kind; the local community can support the programs; local materials can be used for projects. A common commitment increases incentives for higher production. The purpose of such mobilization is twofold: it harnesses previously underused resources, and it economizes on the use of scarce central resources such as administration, transport, and materials.

More resources may be available internationally because meeting the basic needs of the world's poor has stronger moral and political appeal and therefore a higher claim on aid budgets than

34. See Radha Sinha, Peter Pearson, Gopal Kadekodi, and Mary Gregory, *Income Distribution, Growth, and Basic Needs in India* (London: Croom Helm, 1979), chap. 5.

35. For evidence on this, see World Bank, *World Development Report, 1980* (New York: Oxford University Press, 1980), chaps. 4 and 5.

most other schemes advanced for the promotion of international assistance. There can be no certainty about this, but the concept has already attracted international attention and may help to overcome the present coolness toward aid by defining new forms of international cooperation and commitments.[36] Food is an important element in basic needs and, given the distribution of votes in Western democracies, food aid is politically easier than financial aid. Properly channeled so as not to discourage domestic agriculture, food aid can make an important international contribution to meeting basic needs.

It remains to be investigated how a basic needs approach is likely to affect specific resource constraints such as foreign exchange or administrative skills. Although the approach might reduce exports, it would also tend to reduce import requirements, unless domestic food production fails. It would certainly call for more administrative skills, but if local manpower can be harnessed, there would be motivation for increasing the supply of these skills, and if the skills were not particularly sophisticated they could be speedily acquired. The basic needs approach calls for "barefoot" planners and "barefoot" administrators.

In brief, because this approach may save resources, mobilize resources, and make them more productive, it would achieve a given objective sooner than a solely income-oriented approach, even if poverty-weighted. The basic needs resource gap would be narrowed or closed from both ends. The basic needs approach is thrice blessed: it is good in its own right, it raises productivity, and it lowers reproductivity.

Interventions

Government interventions in the market for the purpose of meeting basic needs can be justified on several grounds.

36. A public opinion survey found that although the majority of people do not support general welfare programs, they do support specific measures such as helping poor families with deprived children. Similarly, "aid for development" is less appealing than help in meeting basic needs. A study commissioned by the U.S. Presidential Commission on World Hunger showed that Americans strongly support efforts to alleviate world hunger.

EXTERNALITIES. Many of the core basic needs exhibit externalities in consumption, and some partake of the nature of public goods. In other words, the benefits from one person's consumption are not exhausted by what he pays for it; others benefit too. The elimination of an infectious disease, the acquisition of socially useful skills, sanitation, and even adequate nutrition are examples. Nutrition takes on the characteristics of a public good partly because it contributes to health, which is a public good, and partly because a civilized community does not tolerate the undernourishment of its children. The case for public intervention in such cases is clear.

MARKET IMPERFECTIONS AND INSTITUTIONS. In some basic needs sectors the principal obstacle to success is not lack of resources but certain imperfections in the institutional arrangements within which market forces operate. The poor do not have access to shelter because there are barriers to their acquisition of land, or because titles are uncertain, or because they lack access to mortgage finance. Often the absence of appropriate institutions is the main constraint. For example, primary health care calls for institutions to train and supervise medical auxiliaries, to monitor the distribution of supplies, and to give access to the services of the staff.

CONSUMER EDUCATION. Traditional attitudes, ignorance, or the desire to imitate can be obstacles to meeting basic needs. For instance, improvements in the sanitary and nutritional practices of individuals can greatly reduce the costs of health services and improve the health of the community.

INCOME DISTRIBUTION. Sectoral intervention can be a feasible substitute for the direct redistribution of real income. Nutrition programs for the poor, free education, or targeted price subsidies raise the real incomes of the poor without a change in their nominal income.

SUPPLY MANAGEMENT. Since supplies may respond only slowly or even perversely to market incentives, especially when the needed changes are large, a major change in the pattern of demand may require intervention to secure its objective. According to the basic needs approach, it is not sufficient to channel purchasing power into the hands of the poor by creating employment, raising productivity, improving access to productive factors for the self-employed, and instituting appropriate policies for relative prices. In addition, the structure of production and supply and the institutional arrangements must be capable of responding speedily to the demand generated to meet basic needs.

There are merits in a system that relies on raising the productivity of the poor sufficiently to channel purchasing power to them, and then permits prices and market forces to allocate supplies. No objections in principle are commonly raised against using selective price policies (indirect taxes and subsidies) to steer consumer and producer choices in the direction of meeting basic needs. Prices can be used as an instrument for social objectives. Experience in some countries has shown that attempts to interfere directly with supply by rationing, licensing, issuing building permits, and other direct controls have been open to abuse. At best, they have bred inefficiency and at worst have strengthened monopoly power, increased inequality, and encouraged corruption. Yet it may be necessary to combine the generation of earning opportunities with some form of direct management of supply so that the intentions of the policy are not frustrated. The attempt to raise the productivity of the poor may be frustrated by falling prices of the products they sell. And increasing the money incomes for the poor can be frustrated by rising prices of the goods and services on which they spend their income, if additional supply is not forthcoming. Real incomes do not improve when, for example, improved agricultural prices lead to higher prices of the industrial products bought by farmers. Or the higher money incomes of one group of poor may be met by extra supplies, but only at the expense of diverting supplies from another group which then suffers deprivation.

The disadvantages of rationing and other direct controls have been examined largely in relation to the efficient allocation of resources for productivity and growth, though there has been some work on the effect on employment and income distribution. But there has been hardly any study of the scope and limits of these instruments for meeting basic needs, except under war conditions, A reassessment may well lead to the modification of some of the conclusions.

Changes in relative prices are useful instruments for marginal adjustments, but they are not always equally suitable for bringing about discrete changes. The transition from the present state to a basic needs–oriented approach will call for large and fairly sudden changes. Total prohibition of the import and of the domestic production of a non–basic needs item is often a better way of controlling its consumption (and, indirectly, technology and income distribution) than a tariff combined with an excise tax, if policing to prevent smuggling and bootlegging is effective.[37] Since controls can only prevent activities, not induce them, the positive counterpart to controls may be production in the public sector.

According to one interpretation, the domestic structure of production must be adapted to basic needs requirements. If this were thought to imply forgoing the benefits from foreign trade, such an interpretation would, of course, be nonsense. Supply management may cover, in principle, wholesale and retail distribution, transport and storage, and foreign trade. But a needs-oriented approach may raise previously neglected issues in inter-regional and international trade. Thus, if it were found that the poor in scattered rural communities could not afford to purchase food grains imported from abroad (or produced in the most

---

37. There are arguments other than those of the greater quantitative certainty of quantitative controls. The theoretical assumption that the consumer should be allowed to choose freely according to market prices requires qualification if he can enjoy the product more economically through joint consumption with others; if his satisfaction depends on other people's consumption; if present satisfaction depends partly on what he and others have consumed in the past; and if he does not know what he wants or what is good for him. Some of these often go together. Thus, if each consumer wanted an imported soft drink because others drank it, because he had always drunk it (but would not miss it once he got used to doing without it), and because he overestimated the difficulty of getting the same nutritional value from a local fruit drink, there would be a case for eliminating the imported drink altogether rather than reducing the production of all fruit drinks at the margin or putting a nonprohibitive tax on the import. Analogous assumptions apply to producers.

"efficient" areas domestically) when the costs of transport, distribution, and storage were fully taken into account, it may well turn out that the food should be locally produced, even at what appear to be somewhat higher costs according to calculations that leave out the additional costs.[38]

Supply management has been a controversial issue in the formulation of a basic needs approach. On the one hand, its opponents fear that it would invite an excessive degree of government intervention, which would be at best ineffective, at worst counterproductive, and which would curtail individual freedom. The proponents of supply management, on the other hand, assert that a serious desire to meet basic needs must ensure a structure of production and an organization of the system that will meet the demand of the poor people.

---

38. For evidence on this from Kerala, see United Nations, *Poverty, Unemployment and Development Policy: A Case Study of Selected Issues with Reference to Kerala*, ST/ESA/29 (New York, 1975).

2

The Feasibility of Implementation

THERE CAN BE LITTLE DISAGREEMENT about the priority for meeting basic needs. As an important objective, it follows almost tautologically from the meaning of "basic." The disagreement arises over the feasibility of implementation. Recent work has emphasized the need for low-cost, mass public services, for participation and mobilization of the poor in designing and implementing projects, and for assisting identified groups such as small children and women. It has also brought out the need for experimentation with a wide variety of approaches in the initial stages, to gather experience from pilot projects for replication and, where appropriate, adaptation.

In need of clarification is the question whether meeting basic needs directly is more promising than doing so indirectly. Certain indirect approaches have been discredited,[1] but others remain to be explored. Thus, if the concern is with the poorest 40 percent of the population, would it be better to concentrate on those who are potentially viable farmers, in the hope that their higher production would permit welfare payments for the poorest 10 percent or would generate employment opportunities, or should the needs of the poorest be met directly and immediately? Despite the importance of channeling particular

---

1. For example, one type of trickle-down approach, which concentrates on sectors with high commercial returns and resulting high and concentrated income growth, irrespective of its composition and distribution, on the assumption that the benefits will eventually spread to the poor.

resources to particular groups, some indirect ways of channeling them may be more effective than direct ways.

One inadequacy of past approaches is that they have not done full justice to the precise impact of public services on satisfying needs. In countries where the distribution of incomes, assets, and power is uneven, there is firm evidence that not only private goods but also public services are distributed to the better-off. The incidence of public services reinforces the unequal distribution of private income, and the bias in the provision of essential services has been embedded in the class structure as firmly as the inequality in the consumption of luxury goods in the structure of production. The questions to be investigated are: How can public expenditures on services to meet basic needs be guaranteed to reach the vulnerable groups? How is access to the bureaucracy secured, how are applicants assigned appropriate priorities in the line, and how efficiently are the benefits distributed to those in need? What checks against abuse and what monitoring are required to ensure success?

Social services for the poor and their bias have received a good deal of attention, but the bias of many systems of taxation is equally important. Either taxes do not exist, or nominal taxes are not collected, or, where they are collected, their ultimate incidence is shifted onto others less able to bear them. A thorough scrutiny of the system of collecting revenues and the incidence of taxation is as important for meeting basic needs as the examination of the incidence of public services.

Linkages

The efficacy of the output of one sector—that is, its effect on the length and quality of life—depends largely on the availability of other goods or services that meet basic needs. And since costs can often be reduced by joint supply, there are complementarities both on the side of result and on the side of cost. The impact of investment in sanitation facilities on health depends, for example, on education in personal hygiene; the effectiveness of expenditure on health depends critically on the nature of the output of other basic needs goods. Thus, curative medical services are likely to be rather ineffective if people are chronically malnourished, use germ-infested water, have no sanitation facilities, and follow poor health practices. In some cases, action on one front without simultaneous action on others can be actually counterproductive. To provide water without drainage can lead to stagnant pools that attract insects and spread disease. The improvement of nutrition, of water supply, of sanitation, or of health services, each in isolation, has a smaller effect on the mortality or morbidity of a poverty group than a concerted attack. Without adequate nutrition, resistance to disease will be lower and the cost of a health program higher. Without the elimination of gastrointestinal diseases, nutritional requirements are higher. Without safe water, control of communicable diseases, and improvements in public health, nutritional programs are unlikely to have permanent benefits. There is evidence that family planning programs are more effective if combined with nutrition and health measures. The benefit of education in raising the effectiveness of all other services is obvious. And equally, improved nutrition and health enable children to benefit more from education.

Linkages are important not only in improving the effect of a basic needs program, but also in reducing its costs. Water supply schemes that include the disposal of waste water register lower costs for water and waste disposal combined than if the two types of services are established without regard to one another. In addition, there are important linkages between private income and access to public services. Parents have to earn adequate incomes before they can afford to spare their children from work and send them to school; and they need money to equip them with books, clothes, and transport and to provide them with properly lit rooms for their homework. The sick must be able to afford to travel to clinics.

While a concerted attack on several fronts or a "Big Push" is, therefore, more effective than a sectoral effort, resources are scarce and choices have to be made. Alternatively, there may be scope for substitution between, say, eradicating malaria and some other operation, or between supplying safe water and educating people so that they know when to boil it. In such cases a "vertical" or spearhead approach would be more appropriate than a "horizontal" approach. This implies that the costs and the benefits of these services must be quantified in such a way that selective packages and appropriate phasing can be determined. Costs per unit of a given public service may be reduced if the service is combined with others, and the impact on health, education, nutrition, or family planning may be raised by such a combination. For some purposes "balanced growth," for others an "unbalanced" attack is more economical.[2]

The existence of linkages can lead to reinforcing sequences. Figure 1 illustrates how education influences health status in at least two distinct ways. First, knowledge of hygienic practices improves health. In particular, the education of mothers improves the health of their children. Second, education that raises productivity increases the resources available for meeting basic needs and improving health status. Healthy people, especially children, have a greater capacity for learning, which reinforces the impact of education on health and on productivity. One could add a loop for family planning: higher productivity and earning power and better education encourage family planning; family planning improves nutrition; nutrition improves health; and better health improves attitudes toward family planning. The cumulative and reciprocal nature of these processes shows that policy interventions will have multiplier effects.

The general point is that policies have direct and indirect effects; some reinforce the basic needs objective, others frustrate it. Nutrition policies improve nutrition; health policies, health; and education policies, education. But nutrition policies also affect health and education, as well as the earning power of the poor; health policies affect nutrition, education, and earning power; and education policies affect nutrition, health, and earning power. It may also be that these policies, and the improved productivity of the poor, contribute to the incomes of the better-off. Moneylenders, employers, public officials, and foreign

2. These questions are more fully discussed in chapter 6, with reference to specific experiences.

Figure 1. *Cumulative Causation: Health and Basic Needs*

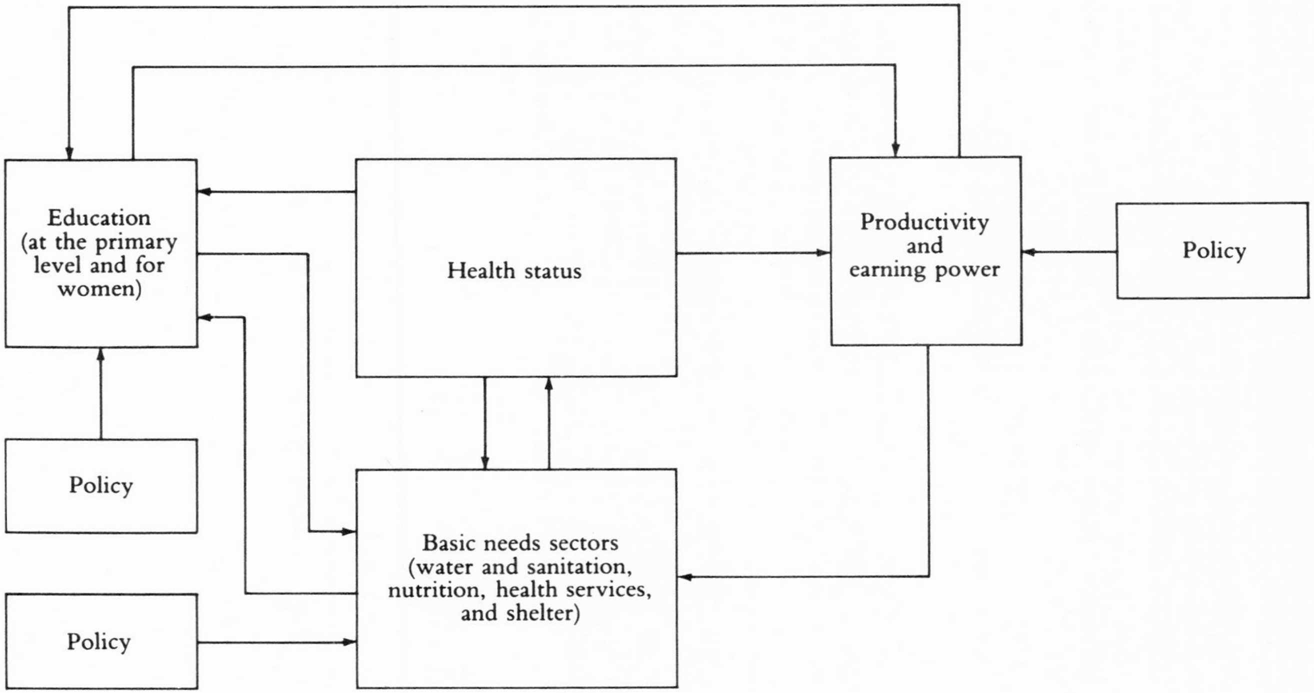

companies may benefit from these improvements, either directly or indirectly. Each of these linkages has a time dimension, so that better education of the poor may lead to higher productivity and to increased incomes of employers, which in turn may give rise to more jobs for the poor. A fully articulated basic needs strategy would have to assess these indirect effects and linkages through time and evolve a set of policies in the light of the basic needs objective.

Technologies and Administration

The cost of providing for basic needs will vary over a wide range, depending on the technology. The technology, in turn, will depend on the degree of local initiative and commitment, the amount and quality of local factors of production and the materials mobilized, and local cultural attitudes and social institutions. The managerial and administrative framework for implementing a basic needs program determines its feasibility and costs. Much is talked about the need for participation and self-management. The important question, however, is how to combine central legislation, central coordination, and central resources with decentralized decisionmaking and the mobilization of local resources (especially underemployed, low-cost labor) to achieve the precise mix that would, in specific circumstances, be most effective. The aim should be to remain adaptable to local needs, but with central power to counter the local elite.

Past calculations for meeting an independently determined range of needs have often started with a head count of those in need and an estimate of the cost of eliminating the deficiency. The counting was often wrong because of a poor data base, and the standards for what was to be supplied were often ill chosen. The resulting bill for "needed services" was exorbitant, and the partial attempts to provide them rarely succeeded in reaching the poor. Planning for basic needs should set standards that are correct and allow for the wide interpersonal and intertemporal variations in human requirements; it should pay attention to what can be afforded by the use of appropriate technologies; it should take account of social and cultural factors, respect indigenous values, mobilize local resources, and concentrate on processes and sequences that meet the needs of the poor. The "count, cost, and deliver" approach has little to contribute to this.[3] Allowing for individual variations in energy requirements, for example, reduces the estimated shortfalls. As P. V. Sukhatme has shown, the incidence of undernutrition in India comes to 25 percent for urban areas and 15 percent for rural areas against the estimates of 50 and 40 percent respectively made by Dandekar and Rath on the basis of a poverty line corresponding to average requirements.[4]

The technology and administration of projects to meet the basic needs of particular deprived groups present special difficulties, in addition to those encountered with more conventional development projects, for at least six reasons:

—Technologically, the methods used (for example, in water supply and waste disposal) may have to be adapted or especially designed to reach the groups.

—Geographically, the vulnerable groups may be remote from the centers of economic activity, adding to problems of transport, communication, and administration.

—Socially and linguistically, the groups may be distinct from those involved in the mainstream of economic activity.

—Politically, the groups may be weak and inarticulate (children have no votes) and may therefore have little power, access to power, or influence on the allocation of resources.

—Economically, the groups may be outside the cash economy and therefore not affected by the forces of economic progress.

—The values held by these groups may be different from those of the planners and administrators, and the setting of objectives and the appraisal of the results of the projects may have

3. The expression "count, cost, and deliver" was coined by Robert Cassen in a background paper to the Brandt Commission.
4. P. V. Sukhatme, *Malnutrition and Poverty*, Ninth Lal Bahadur Shastri Memorial Lecture, January 29, 1977 (New Delhi: Indian Agricultural Research Institute, 1977), p. 16; and V. M. Dandekar and Nilakantha Rath, *Poverty in India* (New Delhi: Ford Foundation, 1970).

to follow criteria that differ from those adopted in the rest of the economy.

Time Discount Rates and Poverty Weighting

Formally, a basic needs strategy can be presented in several different ways. First, a "social welfare function" can be postulated in which welfare is a function of, say, the level and distribution of private and public consumption, and then one can aim at maximizing this "social welfare," subject to the constraint that the basic needs of all must be satisfied.

Second, one may minimize the time in which the basic needs of all should be satisfied. This produces the nonsensible result that even the consumption of the poor must be squeezed to the bare minimum to secure the investment necessary to bring everyone up to the basic needs line in the shortest time.

Third, the number of people who are brought up to the basic needs level may be maximized within a given period. The disadvantage is that the size of the shortfall below basic needs for any given individual is not taken into account. The way to meet this condition is to start with raising the consumption of those just below the line and to dig down gradually until time runs out, leaving the wretched in their wretchedness.

Fourth, after defining a basic needs package (with fixed coefficients between its components) one can maximize the number of packages produced by a certain date. This formulation neglects access and delivery, and tradeoffs between different components of basic needs.

Fifth, one may adhere to a conventional utility function but attach additional weight to minimizing the present value of absolute deprivation (defined as not sustainably meeting basic needs) over time. In the third, fourth, and fifth methods, meeting "basic needs" can be traded off against other objectives, and the absolutism of the first two methods is avoided. Old-fashioned growth maximization[5] is, literally interpreted, a non-

---

5. As in Chenery and others, *Redistribution with Growth*, p. 48.

sensical objective, for it would mean minimum productive consumption and maximum investment until doomsday, when an infinite consumption orgy is let loose.

A distinctive feature of the basic needs approach is a high rate of social time discount for the near future, which reflects the urgency of meeting basic needs soon, subject to maintaining indefinitely the achieved satisfactions. An absolutist and extreme interpretation of the basic needs strategy would be the second model, in which the objective is to minimize the time required to provide everyone with the basic needs basket of goods and services on a sustainable basis. This would imply quite draconian restrictions on groups of people normally regarded as quite poor. Any surplus above the basic needs basket would have to be taxed in order to accumulate the necessary capital to meet everyone's basic needs speedily. This interpretation would also imply an absolute bar on the pursuit of any other objective. No government could be expected to pursue such a policy, and rightly so.

Another distinctive feature of the basic needs approach is the weighting of the needs of those at different distances below the given standard. Previous approaches either simply counted the heads of those below a defined poverty line, without distinguishing degrees of deprivation among them, or attached different weights to income growth of different deciles. A. K. Sen has suggested a weighted measure of the income shortfalls below the basic needs line.[6] He ranks the income of the poor and uses the rank values as weights on the income shortfalls of the different persons in the category of the poor. If there are m people with incomes below the basic needs line, the income shortfall of the richest among the poor gets a weight of 1, the second richest a weight of 2, and so on, ending up with a weight of m on the shortfall of the poorest poor. This measure has the virtue of

6. A. K. Sen, "The Welfare Basis of Real Income Comparisons: A Survey," *Journal of Economic Literature,* vol. 17, no. 1 (March 1979), pp. 1–45; "Economic Development: Objectives and Obstacles," paper presented at the Research Conference on the Lessons of China's Development Experience for the Developing Countries, sponsored by the Social Science Research Council/American Council of Learned Societies, Joint Committee on Contemporary China, San Juan, Puerto Rico, 1976; and *Poverty and Economic Development,* Second Vikram Sarabhai Memorial Lecture, Ahmedabad, December 5, 1976.

being sensitive to the exact pattern of the income shortfalls of the poor from the basic needs line.

But since income is an inadequate and only partial guide to basic needs, it is necessary to supplement the above approach by taking explicit account of which goods and services are going to whom. Again, Sen has suggested that "commodity j going to person i may be thought to be a good ij in itself, not the same as the same commodity going to another person k, which is now taken to be a different good, jk . . . The approach can, of course, be married also to that of dealing with characteristics such as calories as opposed to specific commodities such as rice or bajra."[7] In this manner, weights would be attached not to income but to specific goods and services or even to the impact on specified basic needs.

A pure basic needs approach would give zero weight to meeting the needs of those above the basic needs line, until the basic needs of all were met. But if this approach is regarded as an adjunct to other strategies, the relative weight to be attached to income growth of those above the basic needs line remains to be determined by the policymakers. In a pure basic needs approach, for example, any amount of capital accumulation for non–basic needs would be sacrificed, if doing so would allow the basic needs of all to be satisfied, on a sustainable basis, within a short period. A mixed strategy might prefer to leave the basic needs of 5 percent unsatisfied, if doing so would sustain the growth of income above basic needs for the remaining 95 percent.

The Politics of Basic Needs

It is sometimes argued that basic needs is an ideological concept that conceals a call to revolution. Such an interpretation can

---

7. Sen, *Poverty and Economic Development*, p. 21. The text says *ik*, but this must be a misprint.

8. Others have accused the advocates of basic needs of extreme conservatism—of wishing to arrest developing countries at a low, pastoral stage of development and to prevent radical reforms.

be justified neither historically nor analytically. (Even if it were justified, a "delivery system" would still be required for the revolution.) It is true that the basic needs approach points to actions that go beyond the delivery of a basic package to the poor and include political mobilization. Equally evident is the wide variety of political regimes—such as those of Japan, Israel, Costa Rica, South Korea, Singapore, China, Yugoslavia, Sri Lanka, and others—that have satisfied basic needs within a relatively short time. Options for the future are even more numerous than indicated by the limited experience of the past twenty-five years.

Of course, the success of these different political regimes in meeting basic needs cannot be attributed to their having written basic needs on their banner. But they share certain initial conditions (such as similarities in the distribution of land, tenure systems, and levels of education and health), some of which were indeed established after a revolution, as in China and Cuba, or a war, as in South Korea. They also share policies that present important lessons to others attempting to meet basic needs. That they started from a base at which some basic needs for health and education were already satisfied obviously reduced the time required for meeting basic needs, both directly and, indirectly, through their effect on the quality and motivation of the labor force.

Some countries, such as India, with its "minimum needs" program, and China, adopted basic needs strategies before the term became popular. If some political regimes have succeeded in satisfying basic needs within a short period without adopting the basic needs approach as an explicit policy, others have paid lip service to the objective without succeeding in implementing it. The reasons for this gap between profession and practice are, ultimately, political. To some extent (it might be objected), governments lack the knowledge and administrative power to meet basic needs. Rural development programs are far more difficult to administer than those for the urban elite, though the same governments are often capable of administering complex programs of import restrictions or investment licensing to protect the privileged. The neglect might also be partly explained by the system of incentives and the technology considered essential to a development strategy. It is argued elsewhere in this book that the administrative demands of a basic needs approach are indeed special and complex. But neither administrative weakness nor incentives and technology can fully account for what must ultimately be attributed to the absence of a political base. High marginal tax rates, paid by very few, and land reform legislation that remains unimplemented are the result not so much of administrative weakness or a belief in the need for incentives as of the fact that the rich operate the machinery to their own advantage. The second assumption of the growth strategy—that governments in societies in which power is concentrated have no interest in eradicating poverty—applies with equal force to a basic needs approach. It is not ignorance that has prevented the implementation of anti-poverty programs, nor even lack of political will, but the absence of a political base.[9]

If the failures of past strategies are due to vested interests and to the political obstruction of those who would lose from a basic needs approach, it becomes essential to keep such forces in check. In many regimes the poor are weak bargainers and are not a political constituency. But measures to meet basic needs can be implemented by a reformist alliance, in a peaceful manner. Some of these measures, such as the eradication of communicable diseases or the preservation of social peace, are clearly in the narrow self-interest of the dominant groups. Others are in the long-term interest of some groups who would have to mobilize support for gradual reform. In nineteenth-century England, the rural rich campaigned against the urban rich for factory legislation, which improved the condition of the poor, while the urban rich campaigned against the rural rich for the repeal of the Corn Laws, which reduced the price of food for the poor. Urban industrialists and workers may support a land reform that will benefit small-scale farmers and landless laborers, if it promises

9. Srinivasan has emphasized that the same political and institutional constraints that prevented the benefits of growth from reaching the poor to any significant extent also apply to attempts to provide basic needs. He cites the Indian experience of planning for minimum needs. T. N. Srinivasan, "Development, Poverty, and Basic Human Needs: Some Issues," *Food Research Institute Studies*, vol. 16, no. 2 (1977), pp. 11-28.

more food, which is in the interest of both groups. Concessions to the poor may also be seen as a condition for survival by the ruling elite.

It is possible that the mobilization of the rural and urban masses required for this approach could initiate a revolutionary process, which the initiators of the mobilization process might regret. The conditions which make this liable to happen and which give rise to a grass-roots democracy on a pluralist model have received almost no attention so far.

A basic needs approach calls for decentralization to the village and district level so that plans can be adapted to variable local conditions and the power and efforts of the poor can be mobilized. At the same time, such decentralization often concentrates power in the hands of the local elite, who block policies that would benefit the poor. In the interest of the rural poor, decentralization therefore has to be balanced by the retention of power in the central government. It is not an easy task to design an administrative and political structure which is both decentralized for adaptability and flexibility and centralized explicitly for the protection of the poor and the politically weak. Voluntary organizations can also make an important contribution by offering guidance to local leaders on the special needs of the poor.

The main conclusion of this section is that government policy must be seen neither as entirely above the economic and social forces, directing them in the manner of Platonic guardians, nor simply as the expression of the self-interest of the ruling class. Rather, it is itself one of the dependent variables that can be shaped and improved by the other variables of the social system, especially by reformist coalitions.

Problems of Transition

A major difficulty of a basic needs approach is that efforts to meet basic needs in a short time, in a society that previously pursued non–basic needs policies, will create disequilibrium in several markets, with macroeconomic repercussions. It is not easy to change the structure of production quickly, to beat non–basic needs swords into basic needs plowshares, or to stop construction of non–basic needs projects abruptly.

As demand is redirected toward basic needs goods in inelastic supply (especially food, but also other basic goods), their prices will tend to rise and imports will tend to increase. The income elasticity of demand for food among the poor can be as high as 0.7, whereas the short-run supply elasticity of food grains is about 0.1 or 0.2. As the recipients of the now higher incomes find that the intentions of the policy are being frustrated, they will demand higher money incomes. If these demands are successful, inflationary pressures will mount.

As the demand for non–basic needs luxury goods is reduced, their prices are not likely to fall, but production will be cut back and unemployment will rise. These luxury goods are not likely to find foreign markets, for they will tend to have been produced at uncompetitive costs behind protective barriers. A combination of wage-price inflation (possibly reinforced by the financial system), unemployment, and a balance of payments crisis will plague the country. The rise in the price of food may be particularly hard on poor food consumers in distant and isolated communities and on vulnerable individuals in commercialized communities with transport and communication links to the markets.

The contraction of demand in the existing manufacturing sector and the reduction on the rate of profit may lead to a collapse in private investment. Upper income groups, when their interests are threatened, will attempt to take their capital out of the country, and professionals may wish to leave. Disaffected groups may go on strike, and the opposition may even mount coups d'état.

These damaging repercussions on stability, employment, and the balance of payments can be reduced if the government announces clearly and firmly the measures it proposes to take (for example, the taxation of higher incomes) and generates the confidence that it will abide by them. The detrimental effects, such as the collapse of private investment and capital flight, stem partly from the uncertainty created by the transition period, and if this uncertainty is reduced, resources can be reallocated with minimal damage.

Difficulties such as these point to the need for some supply management, analogous to that practiced during the transition from a peacetime to a wartime economy. There are implications for international aid in such a reorientation (discussed in chapter 8), but the political economy of the transition and the political, administrative, and institutional problems that it raises are among the most difficult issues of a basic needs approach.

Some Unresolved Issues

The preceding discussion has probably raised many doubts in the reader's mind. One question might be: Who is to determine the basic needs? Is it the people themselves, who may prefer circuses to bread, television to education, or soft drinks, beer, and cigarettes to clean water and carrots? Would it not be very arrogant to lay down what people should regard as basic?

There is conflicting evidence on the connection between the choices actually made by the poor and basic needs as determined by nutritionists and doctors. From Seebohm Rowntree's study of poverty in York at the turn of the century to a World Bank report on human resources in Brazil, it is clear that many people, in spite of adequate incomes to buy the products that would keep them well nourished and healthy, do in fact spend their money on other things and therefore suffer.[10] Rowntree (p. 86) referred to "secondary poverty," a condition in which "earnings would be sufficient for the maintenance of merely physical efficiency were it not that some portion of it is absorbed by other expenditure, either useful or wasteful" such as drink, gambling, and inefficient housekeeping. Secondary poverty prevented many more people from meeting what he called a "human needs standard" than did primary poverty (that is, inadequate incomes).

10. B. Seebohm Rowntree, *Poverty: A Study of Town Life* (London: Macmillan, 1901); and Peter T. Knight and others, "Brazil: Human Resources Special Report" (Washington, D.C.: World Bank, 1979; processed).

Similarly, evidence from Brazil shows that malnutrition is wide-spread in spite of incomes that are adequate to buy the essential food. There is also evidence, however, that some very poor people often get good value from their expenditure. It might well be that the deviations arise as people become better off and subject to the pressures of advertisers, the demonstration effect, and emulation.

It is difficult to envisage any society in which the five basic needs sectors discussed in this book—nutrition, education, health, shelter, water and sanitation—would not be contained in the definition of basic needs, even if all five sectors did not require improvement. But these five core basic needs may not coincide with the list of basic needs expressed by the people. They would probably give high priority to personal safety, which would lead to a demand for more police protection, more secure prisons, and so on. The ILO considers employment a basic need; Sidney Webb would include leisure. High on the list, as China recognized in the six guarantees, is a decent funeral, for which working-class people in England are prepared to pay large insurance premiums. Other needs that would be given priority are various forms of patent medicines and barbiturates, television, ownership of land for peasants, a grand wedding, national glory, and sexual gratification.

As soon as the question of who determines basic needs is raised, another ambiguity in the literature becomes apparent. Do basic needs refer to the conditions for a full, long, and healthy life, or to a specified bundle of goods and services that are deemed to provide the opportunity for these conditions? The fact is that very little is known about the causal links between the provision of specific items and the achievement of a full life. Planning ministries, donor agencies, and some intellectuals tend to prefer the technocratic approach, in which the bundle is specified, costed, and delivered. But this approach is not only incompatible with respect for human autonomy, but also ineffective or very costly.

The foregoing discussion raises the problem of participation, a concept often used as a slogan, without careful consideration of precisely what is implied. First, there is the question of the purpose of participation: Is it personal satisfaction, work enrichment, greater efficiency to improve results or lower costs, community development, or the promotion of solidarity? Is it an end or a means, and if a means, to what ends? What if there are conflicts between these objectives? Can participation deal effectively with strategic decisions, or even with tactical managerial ones?

Second, what form should participation take? At a factory, it might take the form of codetermination of policy, work councils, shop-floor participation, financial participation, or collective bargaining. It could even be argued that the market is a form of participation. In basic needs projects there are similarly many forms, and it would have to be spelled out which is appropriate for which objective. Participation would have to be fitted into the apparatus of development administration, with decentralized decisionmaking supported by decisions at intermediate and central levels. What central support is needed to give effect to participation? Is there a case for central action to counteract local self-determination, if it works against the interests of the poor because powerful members of the local community have taken over?

Third, what is the relation between participation and democratic institutions? The corporate state under various forms of fascism encouraged the participation of organized groups of employers, workers, and farmers, and it is said that Tito and other socialist dictators got the idea of self-managed enterprises from Mussolini. China has practiced mass participation on a grand scale. Participation can be used to bypass elected members of parliament and can be highly undemocratic. Devolution of important decisions to local bodies may mean handing power to members of the local power elite who grind the faces of the poor. Central decisionmaking often provides safeguards for the interests of the poor.

Fourth, the "representatives" of organized groups are normally more ambitious, more vocal, more capable, better educated, and often better-off than the people they represent. Such highly unrepresentative leaders may lack the ability to identify local needs and aspirations, and it is not at all clear that they should be the ones to formulate the priority and content of basic needs. Nor is it clear how to avoid the twin dangers of elitist dictation or consciousness-raising from above and the nonarticulation of basic needs from below.

Fifth, when do people have a right to participate in decisions that importantly affect their lives? "If four men propose marriage to a woman, her decision about whom, if any of them, to marry importantly affects each of the lives of these four persons, her own life, and the lives of any other persons wishing to marry one of these four men, and so on."[11] Yet, no one would propose that all these people should vote to decide whom she should marry. Certain rights set limits to participation, however important the decision may be for those excluded. In the light of these questions, it is preferable to spell out the administrative structure necessary for an efficient implementation of a basic needs approach.

Another area of doubt concerns the possibility that at least one of the objections raised to the growth approach may also apply to the basic needs approach. It may be agreed that the effects of growth do not trickle down, or do so only slowly or unreliably, and that it is not necessary to keep the consumption of the poor down for a long time to accumulate enough capital to meet the needs of the poor. But if governments show resistance to redistributing the fruits of growth widely, are they not likely to resist meeting basic needs? Of course, removing absolute poverty is different from promoting equality, and meeting the basic needs of the poor—feeding the hungry, clothing the naked, and succoring the sick—has a much stronger appeal than do egalitarian policies. Basic needs policies need not hurt the interests of the rich in the way that redistribution does. And it is easier to implement such policies at an early stage of development than later, when concentrated growth has created powerful interests. But it might be objected that a radical implementation of a basic needs approach is liable to run into the same obstacles and inhibitions as policies of redistribution do.

11. Robert Nozick, *Anarchy, State, and Utopia* (New York: Basic Books, 1974), p. 269.

This raises the question whether a basic needs approach calls for a radical or even a revolutionary strategy, or whether it is merely a palliative. Those who believe the latter say that it attacks symptoms rather than causes. It can be argued that palliatives may be the best that can be achieved and that the alternative is not more radical reform but doing nothing at all for the poor.

There are two objections to this line of argument. First, unless the palliative can be sustained, it may undermine the possibility of continuing the relief and may prepare the ground for worse problems later. Second, the policies to implement palliatives may preclude other changes that would have eradicated poverty more efficiently and more lastingly. Improvements that are unambiguous by the criteria of welfare economics may bar other improvements in income distribution and factor allocation, which would have been better still.

Karl Marx said, "Philosophers have *interpreted* the world, in various ways; the point, however, is to *change* it."[12] And Albert Hirschman has discussed the relation between the advance in our understanding of a problem and in our motivation to tackle it. In tackling basic needs the question is whether our desire to change the world has not run ahead of our correct interpretation and understanding. "The lag of understanding behind motivation is likely to make for a high incidence of mistakes and failures in problem-solving activities and hence for a far more frustrating path to development than the one" in which understanding paces ahead of motivation.[13]

Critical readers might think that basic needs as an objective is noncontroversial, and that the approaches, policies, or strategies implied by the term are not different from those of "growth with equity," or "growth with poverty alleviation," or "redistribution with growth." Indeed, many of the architects of the success stories quoted in this book would be surprised if they were told that they had pursued a basic needs approach. Other critics might

---

12. "Theses on Feuerbach," in Karl Marx and Fredrick Engels, *Selected Works* (Moscow: Foreign Languages Publishing House, 1958), p. 405.

13. Albert O. Hirschman, *Journeys Toward Progress* (New York: Twentieth Century Fund, 1963), pp. 237-38.

say that even in the most affluent countries the basic needs of many are not met, and that we do not know how to attack and eradicate poverty.

It might also be said that the obstacle is not a lack of understanding but a lack of motivation on the part of those in power. Is it stupidity or cupidity, ignorance or "lack of political will" (or lack of a political base) that prevents the eradication of poverty? Later chapters throw some light on these perennial questions, without answering them definitively.

Another unsettled issue is the relation between meeting basic needs as an end in itself and as an instrument for developing human resources. The argument of this book is that human development is, above all, good in itself. If the consumption of radios, bicycles, TV, and beer is accepted as desirable, there is no reason not to accept better health and education as at least equally desirable. Not only is the development of human resources desirable in itself, but it also raises productivity and lowers reproductivity. The consumption aspects and the investment aspects of human resource development thus reinforce each other. Why, then, should the human resource developers who emphasize productivity and the humanitarians who emphasize the intrinsic value of human development not be in alliance instead of at loggerheads, as they so often are? If education, for example, is shown to be productive, as well as good in its own right, should the educators not embrace the economists and regard their arguments as strengthening the case for spending more on education? The same goes for health and other forms of social expenditure.

Unfortunately, a harmony of interests between human resource developers and humanitarians cannot be established so easily. Choices have to be made, and these choices are liable to depend on whether humanitarianism or productivity is the overriding concern. Conflicts may arise with respect to the beneficiaries and the content of the human resource development.

First, some human beings are not and never will be members of the labor force: the old, the disabled, the permanently sick. Are these unemployables to be beneficiaries of a basic needs approach? It has been argued that resources devoted to this group also have a positive effect on production, and a negative effect on reproduction. If an important motive for having children is to provide for old age or infirmity, a social commitment to look after the old and infirm will remove this motive and reduce the size of family that is desired. Aside from such possible overlaps, however, there is a clear conflict between those who would emphasize exclusively productivity and those who would emphasize humanity.

Second, choices must be made about the content of the investment in human capital. Should education be general, so as to give access to the store of human civilization, or should it be technical, so as to improve working skills? Should it be liberal or scientific, pure or applied? Should it be formal or informal, in institutions or on the job? These various forms are likely to be different in their intrinsic desirability and their consequences for production. Even the most narrowly productivity-oriented human developer will have to admit that education should not be identified solely with schooling, and health not solely with medical services (expenditure on health services more often measures the health of the health services than the health of the people). It would be a strange fluke, however, if the type of education desired by humanitarian educators is precisely the same as that desired by the proponents of economic growth.

Third, there may be differences in the time horizon. The proportion of resources devoted to primary, secondary, and tertiary education, and the choice of educating children, youths, or adults, are partly dictated by technical relations. There is a need to train teachers and administrators even if the principal emphasis is on primary education, and there is a need to educate parents if high drop-out rates from primary schools are to be avoided. But the choice is also partly determined by a different time horizon: whether the primary goal is to improve the existing labor force or, through investment in children, the future labor force.

Fourth, the treatment of human investment in a particular group will differ according to whether the emphasis is on the development of autonomous human beings or on their contribution to increased production. In the education of women, conflicts will tend to arise between those who stress women's freedom of choice—their need for more earning opportunities and equality with men in pay and access to jobs—and those who emphasize better services in the home and family, such as improved nutrition and hygiene for children. The implications for breast feeding, for example, are quite different in the two approaches. The pleas of the women's liberation movement are in conflict with the pleas of those who call for an improvement in the specifically feminine roles of wife and mother.

It must therefore be concluded that a pure basic needs approach may conflict with a productivity and growth approach, although the two approaches overlap in some areas.

Also open to criticism are the methods employed to show that investment in human capital has favorable effects on economic growth. Econometric exercises establishing correlations between social and human indicators, such as life expectancy, literacy, and infant mortality on the one hand, and growth rates on the other, give no clue to the causal relations. Good nutritional levels are related to higher incomes and higher incomes to higher growth rates of GNP, but it would be misleading to conclude that better nutrition therefore makes for faster economic growth. Microstudies of the impact of investment in humans on their productivity are inconclusive because success for one group may be at the expense of other groups outside the map of the study. Thus, raising the money incomes of some members of the poorest 30 percent may push up the price of food and further impoverish the remainder. Yet, the combination of econometric studies and microstudies makes a persuasive case for human development as an influence on productivity and growth.

3

The Search for
a Suitable Yardstick

To IMPLEMENT A BASIC NEEDS APPROACH, a system of monitoring the satisfaction of basic human needs is needed. Highly sophisticated economic indicators have been developed, but the human and social indicators required for a basic needs approach are still primitive.

Ever since economists have attempted to tackle development problems, the principal yardsticks for measuring economic development have been GNP, its components, and their growth. Despite the many problems with national accounting in developing countries, the national accounts have continued to be the main framework for discussions of growth, the allocations between investment, consumption, and saving, and the relative influence of various sectors in total value added. GNP per head is widely accepted as the best single indicator of development, both historically and for international comparisons.

The use of national accounting was inspired by the attention of economists to the broad aggregates of Keynesian economics, which was itself a major influence on economic thought in the 1950s, when the less developed countries began to enter the limelight. Through a weighting system based on market prices or factor costs, national accounting served to integrate such disparate items as agriculture and industrial production, investment, consumption, and government services. In fact, national income accounting was a tool of analysis that other social scientists sometimes viewed with considerable envy. The heavy emphasis on using GNP, or GNP per head, and their growth rates as the principal tests of the performance (not normally as the objective) of welfare or development came under fire for the reasons given in chapter 1.

The concern has now shifted to the eradication of absolute poverty, particularly by concentrating on basic human needs. The needs for nutrition, education, health, and shelter may be met through various combinations of policies to promote growth, redistribute assets and income, restructure production, and reduce population growth. The composition of production and its beneficiaries have become more significant than indexes of total production or of income distribution. This new emphasis on meeting basic human needs requires an indicator or a set of indicators which can be used to judge and measure deprivation and to initiate and monitor policies directed at its alleviation and eradication.

The problems inherent in using GNP as a measure of social welfare have been recognized almost since the inception of national income accounting. This chapter identifies and reviews four different approaches to the measurement problem: (1) adjustments to GNP, by which standard concepts of national income accounting are modified to capture some of the welfare aspects of development and to improve international comparability; (2) social indicators, which attempt to define nonmonetary measures of social progress; (3) the related social accounting systems, which attempt to provide an organizing framework for some of the social indicators; and (4) the development of composite indexes, which combine various social indicators into a single index of human and social development or of the "quality of life." In addition to these four broad approaches, efforts have been made to design an adequate measure of income distribution and to count the number of people living below a defined poverty line. This is briefly discussed in the following section. The extensive literature on this subject could, however, warrant a separate review.[1]

_____

1. A fifth method would be to interview a sample of individuals and to ask each to place himself on a happiness or basic needs scale between, for example, zero and ten, and to say whether his basic needs were being met more adequately than at some specified date in the past. But this kind of survey is still rudimentary and does not provide the kind of information needed to monitor a basic needs approach.

Adjustments to the GNP Measure

Despite the overwhelming attention to growth, the deficiencies of GNP per head as an indicator of economic development became apparent to many, even during the early years. Pigou had pointed out in 1920 that economic welfare comprises not only national income per head but also its distribution and the degree of its steadiness of fluctuation over time.[2] Measurement problems became apparent in the attempt to make intercountry comparisons of GNP per head. Part of the problem arises from the fact that official exchange rates do not measure relative domestic purchasing power, since a large portion of marketed GNP does not enter into world trade. In addition, trade policies often create distortions in nominal exchange rates, so that they fail to reflect the true value of even that proportion of GNP which is traded.

Clark was one of the first to attempt to convert national accounts by the use of purchasing power parities.[3] This means measuring the output of each country at a common price level, usually international prices. The most recent and complete work on purchasing power parities has been undertaken by Kravis and others.[4] The results of this research suggest that the GNP of India, for instance, should be adjusted upward by a factor of 3.5, while that of most other countries would be adjusted by a somewhat smaller margin. Even these kinds of adjustment, however, cannot eliminate all the problems of comparing GNP among countries. For instance, climatic conditions may require greater expenditure for clothing and shelter in the more temperate parts of the world, while dry tropical zones require more expenditure on irrigation and disease control. Evaluations of nontradables, par-

2. A. C. Pigou, *The Economics of Welfare*, 1st ed. (London: Macmillan, 1920).
3. Colin Clark, *Conditions of Economic Progress*, 3d ed. (London: Macmillan, 1951).
4. Irving B. Kravis, Zoltan Kenessey, Alan Heston, and Robert Summers, *A System of International Comparisons of Gross Product and Purchasing Power* (Baltimore, Md.: Johns Hopkins University Press, 1975); and Irving B. Kravis, Alan Heston, and Robert Summers, *International Comparisons of Real Product and Purchasing Power* (Baltimore, Md.: Johns Hopkins University Press, 1978).

ticularly public and other services, are difficult and subject to conceptual problems. In addition, a great deal of work is necessary to cover hundreds of goods and services for an accurate estimate of purchasing power parities. Unless a short cut or a reduced information approach is developed, it would be difficult to make wide use of this method.

Nordhaus and Tobin attempted to adjust GNP so that it would be a better measure of economic welfare (MEW).[5] They subtracted from GNP an allowance for defense expenditures and other "regrettable necessities," such as the "disamenities" of urbanization (pollution, congestion, and crime), and added an estimate of the value of leisure and the services of consumer durables. At the same time, Nordhaus and Tobin reclassified health and education expenditures as investment, rather than consumption. The final result produced a MEW for the United States that was about twice as large as GNP, mainly because the high value imputed to leisure (the measure of which raises great difficulties) and other nonmarket activities. The growth rate of MEW for the United States between 1929 and 1965 was somewhat lower than that for GNP, mainly because the larger value of leisure and nonmarket activities in the base year (1929) reduced the proportionate rate of growth, and partly because of the growth of defense expenditure and urban disamenities. Denison and others have criticized this approach on the ground that GNP was never meant to measure welfare, and attempts to adjust it only confuse the concept.[6]

GNP adjustments might be able to incorporate some of the items captured by social indicators. Thus, life expectancy could be allowed for by using expected lifetime earnings instead of annual income per head or, more crudely, the product of average income per head and life expectancy. The consumption benefits of literacy could be allowed for by imputing the value of services from education as a durable consumer good. (The benefits of

5. William D. Nordhaus and James Tobin, "Is Growth Obsolete?" in *Economic Growth* (New York: Columbia University Press for NBER, 1972); see also Wilfred Beckerman, *Two Cheers for the Affluent Society* (New York: St. Martin's Press, 1974), chap. 4.

6. Edward F. Denison, "Welfare Measurement and the GNP," *Survey of Current Business*, vol. 51, no. 1 (January 1971), pp. 13-16.

literacy as a durable investment good already show in the form of higher productivity.) Distribution could be allowed for by taking the median or the mode rather than the mean income, which gives excessive weight to the few very rich, or by multiplying the mean income by 1 minus the Gini coefficient.[7]

There are certain difficulties in using the Nordhaus-Tobin corrections to indicate the satisfaction of basic needs. "Regrettable necessities" are subtracted from GNP because "we see no direct effect of defense expenditures on household economic welfare. No reasonable country (or household) buys 'national defense' for its own sake. If there were no war or risk of war, there would be no need for defense expenditures and no one would be the worse without them." But similar reasoning could be applied to the components of basic needs. Medical services from nurses, doctors, and hospitals are not desired for their own sake; if it were not for disease and accidents, there would be no need to incur this expenditure. The same goes for shelter against the cold, for sewerage, and perhaps for literacy. Even food for under- or malnourished people is a necessity to prevent hunger, disease, or death. A logically consistent application of the Nordhaus-Tobin principle would include in the national income only those items that are not really needed—the inessentials and frills. This paradoxical conclusion would be contrary to the judgment of those who wish to *exclude* all frivolous luxuries from national income accounts.[8]

If it were possible to distinguish precisely between "goods," "bads," and "anti-bads," one could deduct from national income all "anti-bads": expenditures on defense to combat the "bads" generated by potential enemies, expenditures on heating, shelter, and medicines to offset the "bads" generated by nature—

7. See A. K. Sen, "Economic Development: Objectives and Obstacles," paper presented at the Research Conference on the Lessons of China's Development Experience for the Developing Countries, sponsored by the Social Science Research Council/American Council of Learned Societies, Joint Committee on Contemporary China, San Juan, Puerto Rico, 1976.

8. Since in the absence of desires and wants there would be no need for the goods to satisfy them, the national income might be by definition zero if this line of reasoning were carried to its logical conclusion.

the narrowest definition of basic needs; and expenditures to offset the "bads" generated by the domestic economic system itself, which "artificially" creates wants through advertising, social pressures, and industrial pollution. In fact, it is not possible to distinguish between good and bad artificially created wants without introducing value judgments; the desire for books, art, and music is also artificially created. Nor is it possible to distinguish between "anti-bads" (the need for deodorants or anti-dandruff shampoo created by the fear of social ostracism) and "goods" (the need for literature created by the desire to participate in the cultural life of society).

Adjustments to GNP for distributional value judgments can be made by weighting different components of the national income according to who receives them. Such a redefinition would, however, eliminate the distinction between the national income and its distribution. Kuznets and Ahluwalia and Chenery have suggested that the growth rate of GNP in itself is a misleading indicator of development, since it is heavily weighted by the income shares of the rich.[9] A growth of 10 percent in incomes of the richest 20 percent of the population will have a greater effect on the aggregate growth rate than will a 10 percent growth in incomes of the poorest 20 percent. They suggest either the equal weighting of each decile of income recipients or the introduction of "poverty weights," which would place more weight on the growth of incomes for the poorest 40 percent. The result is a revised aggregate growth rate that allows for differences and changes in income distribution.

Another approach would simply use the absolute income level of the poorest 40 percent as the appropriate indicator of the satisfaction of basic needs. This measure has the advantage of shifting the focus from the distribution of income, a politically sensitive subject in many countries, to the level of living of the

9. Simon Kuznets, "Problems in Comparing Recent Growth Rates for Developed and Less Developed Countries," *Economic Development and Cultural Change*, vol. 20, no. 2 (January 1972), pp. 185-209; and Montek S. Ahluwalia and Hollis Chenery, "The Economic Framework," in Hollis Chenery and others, *Redistribution with Growth* (London: Oxford University Press, 1974), pp. 38-51.

poor. Progress in reducing poverty can be judged, however, only if the income level of the poor can be compared with some standard minimum which constitutes a poverty line. A common approach is to calculate the cost of a "minimal" nutritionally balanced diet for an"average" person and then to calculate the ratio of food expenditure to total expenditure. The diet costs are multiplied by the reciprocal of this ratio to allow for expenditure on nonfood items. Those families or individuals whose income is insufficient to cover these minimal expenditures are judged to be below the poverty line and in the poverty target group.

Among the many shortcomings of this approach, the examination of family income and food consumption ignores the important problem of distribution of food and other amenities both among different families below the poverty line and within a family. In many countries women (who may work harder than men) and children receive less than an adequate amount of food, although the family's total consumption may be judged to be "adequate." Poverty line measures do not consider how far below the line families may be, nor do they show improvements that take place below this line. They suggest that a "solution" has been found for those brought barely above the line. They therefore conceal the efforts required to reduce poverty. Sen has proposed weighting individuals on the basis of how far below the poverty line they fall, a suggestion combining poverty line and income distribution approaches.[10]

In addition, a nutritionally adequate diet is difficult to define since caloric needs vary widely with climate, body weight, activity, height, age, and other factors, and even for the same conditions between persons and for the same person in the same conditions from day to day. Household income surveys generally show that many families below the poverty line could consume an adequate diet by purchasing a different basket of foods, but the more nutritious foods available are rejected on grounds of

10. A. K. Sen, "Poverty, Inequality, and Unemployment," *Economic and Political Weekly*, vol. 8, special no. 31-33 (August 1973); reprinted as "Poverty: An Ordinal Approach to Measurement," *Econometrica*, vol. 44, no. 2 (March 1976); and *Poverty and Economic Development*, Second Vikram Sarabhai Memorial Lecture, Ahmedabad, December 5, 1976.

taste, variety, habit, and so on. Families living below the poverty line often spend on nonbasic items, such as drink and entertainment. Even with an income above the poverty line, a family may not be able to purchase essential goods and services (such as health, education, water) that are in short supply or controlled by the public sector. It may have to rely on less efficient and more costly alternatives such as traditional healers, private water deliveries, or private schools. The importance of the public sector in these areas derives from the view that these goods and services meet "merit wants," that is, the government judges them to be more important than consumers would judge them to be, and also derives from the "external economies": the benefits accrue not only to the individual consumer but also to others. The basic needs approach, in fact, stems from the experience that raising incomes alone is insufficient because of inefficiencies in the consumption pattern of the poor and the lack of some essential goods and services. Therefore, any measure of poverty income, no matter how carefully derived, will be inadequate for measuring basic needs.

Two final questions are whether the poverty line should move upward with rising average income, and whether the number or the proportion of the poor below the line is the same or a changing group of individuals.

Social Indicators

Another approach is to develop better indicators of human, social, and economic development that cover areas not reflected in most income-based measures. These so-called social indicators attempt to measure the development of health, nutrition, housing, income distribution, and other cultural and social factors. Various agencies—including the United Nations, OECD, USAID, and Unesco—have put a great deal of work into compiling a set of social indicators.[11]

11. United Nations, Economic and Social Council (ECOSOC), Committee for Development Planning, "Developing Countries and Levels of Development" (New York,

(Note continues on p. 76.)

Social indicators are more useful in cross-country comparisons, since they avoid the problems of exchange rates and valuation. But the statistical basis for comparing these indicators between countries or over time remains very frail. The figures are often unreliable and not comparable because different definitions are used. Many data are based on limited sample surveys or other highly inaccurate methods of data collection. Differences observed in social indicators between countries often reflect these statistical and definitional variations rather than real differences in social development. But this constitutes a challenge to collect better, more comparable data.

Although the pricing mechanism is used to combine heterogeneous items in the national accounts, there is no obvious way to combine different social indicators. Consequently, problems arise in absorbing the content of a large number of socioeconomic indicators and in attempting to draw general conclusions. Furthermore, the movement to develop social indicators has lacked a clear sense of purpose. The term "social indicators" itself very loosely encompasses a whole range of human, economic, social, cultural, and political indicators. The need to supplement the GNP as an indicator of economic development has become confused with a search for indicators of other aspects of development as well as of the "quality of life." The latter concept has generally been taken to cover concepts such as security, peace, equality of opportunity, participation, and personal satisfaction, all of which present difficult problems of measurement. It has never been clear whether the search was for an alternative, a complement, or a supplement to GNP.

Even without a unifying conceptual framework, and despite the problems mentioned above, social indicators do have certain advantages over GNP per head. First, they are concerned with

October 15, 1975); Organisation for Economic Co-operation and Development (OECD), Development Assistance Committee, "Socio-economic Typologies or Criteria and Their Usefulness in Measuring Development Progress" (Paris, April 7, 1977); U.S. Agency for International Development (USAID), "Socio-economic Performance Criteria for Development" (Washington, D.C., February 1977); and United Nations Educational, Scientific and Cultural Organization (Unesco), *The Use of Socio-Economic Indicators in Development Planning* (Paris, 1976).

ends as well as means, or at least with intermediate ends nearer to the ultimate end of a full and healthy life than are aggregate measures of average production. Even those social indicators that measure inputs (such as hospital beds per thousand population or school enrollment rates) rather than results (life expectancy, morbidity, literacy) attempt to capture inputs that are nearer to the desirable results than GNP per head.

Second, many social indicators say something about the distribution as well as the average, because the upper end is less skewed than it is for income per head. (The mode or the median for income per head can, however, eliminate skewness and reflect some aspects of distribution in the average.) There is practically no limit to how much income a man can receive, but the maximum life span is limited. Any increase in literacy reflects also a rough distributional improvement because the *proportion* of beneficiaries has risen.

Some indicators are better than others for showing the distribution of basic deficiencies since they are based on the presence or absence of certain conditions. Thus, measures of literacy, access to clean water, and primary school enrollment can indicate the percentage of the population with deficiencies in each of these important sectors. Measures such as life expectancy, infant mortality, and average caloric consumption are less informative since they average the statistics of rich and poor alike. There seems to be a clear need to develop more specific measures related to the poor, such as indicators of life expectancy or caloric consumption of those in the lower quintile of the income distribution, of women, of rural dwellers, and so on.

Third, while GNP per head follows an ascending order from the poorest to the richest countries, some social indicators are capable of catching something of the human, social, and cultural costs of opulence (such as heart disease, stomach ulcers, or deaths in automobile accidents) as well as of poverty. They can, in principle, register some of the shared global problems, such as pollution and cultural dependence or interdependence, and reduce the false hierarchical and paternalistic impression that may be created by purely economic indicators. As a result, a different meaning can be attached to the so-called gap between the developed and developing countries. The GNP measure points to "catching up" and suggests a race. Social indicators can point to common and shared values and problems, to alternative styles of development, to the opportunities for learning from one another. Reducing or closing the international gap in life expectancy, literacy, infant mortality, or morbidity would appear to be a more sensible objective, and can be achieved at much lower levels of GNP per head and therefore much sooner, than reducing the income gap, though even less is known about how to achieve the former than the latter.

Inputs versus Results

Whether indicators of social and basic needs should reflect inputs or results depends on their purpose. For testing performance there is something to be said for choosing indexes that measure results, impact, or outputs, since these are closer to the ultimate objective. Furthermore, measures of inputs can introduce biases toward certain patterns of meeting needs which may not be universal. For instance, a country with fairly acceptable health standards should not be encouraged to acquire the same number of doctors as one with serious health problems: "regrettable necessities" should not be counted as final goods or as social achievements.

Another drawback is that the number of doctors does not measure the distribution of these doctors and of medical services or the degree of their specialization. Resources may be deployed in inefficient ways and fail to benefit the poor. In contrast, measures such as infant mortality and life expectancy indicate the degree to which basic needs have been fulfilled. Similarly, literacy measures the effectiveness of the educational system and is a better indicator than the number of students enrolled or the student-teacher ratio. In general, measures of output are better indicators of the level of welfare and the satisfaction of basic needs.

Most outputs are also inputs. Health, education, and even nutrition are valued not only in their own right, but also because they raise the productivity of present and future workers; higher productivity in turn is valued because it contributes to a better life.

Input measures, such as doctors or hospital beds per thousand population or enrollment rates in schools, also have their uses, however. They may reflect government intention, commitment, and efforts to provide public services. To assess policies and monitor performance, both sets of indicators are necessary. Input measures are useful indicators of the resources devoted to certain objectives (though the resources can be misdirected). To the extent to which inputs can be linked to results, that is, inputs have a known "production function," the connections between means and ends can be traced. Even without knowledge of a production function (as in the case of the links between expenditure on family planning and a decline in the fertility rate), the combination of input and output measures presents the raw material for research into the causal links between the two, particularly since, in a social system of interdependent variables, many outputs are also inputs. In addition, when output measures cannot be readily found, it might be necessary to fall back on measures of inputs as useful proxies.

GNP versus Social Indicators

Several studies have suggested that since rankings of countries by GNP and by social indicators are very similar, GNP can be used as a proxy measure of social development.[12] Morawetz found that there was a weak correlation between the level of GNP and indicators of basic needs fulfillment, and even less correlation between the growth of GNP and improvements in basic needs indicators.[13] Sheehan and Hopkins concluded, however, that "the most important variable explaining the average level of

12. D. V. McGranahan, Claude Richaud-Proust, N. V. Sovani, and Muthu Subramanian, *Contents and Measurement of Socio-Economic Development* (New York: Praeger, 1972); and ECOSOC, "Developing Countries and Levels of Development."

13. David Morawetz, *Twenty-five Years of Economic Development, 1950 to 1975* (Baltimore, Md.: Johns Hopkins University Press, 1977).

basic needs satisfaction is per capita gross national product.''[14] These contradictory results appear to arise from the selection of different indicators, sources of data, and country samples, as well as different interpretations of results. Many scholars include in social indicators such nonmonetary measures of economic performance as the consumption of newsprint or energy or the ownership of automobiles and radios. These economic indicators are almost always highly correlated with GNP, and at times they have been suggested as a shortcut to estimating internationally comparable income levels.[15] Some authors exclude the developed countries because their high levels of GNP and social development might dominate the sample. Different results are obtained with the inclusion or exclusion of the centrally planned economies, the OPEC countries, and the very small developing countries.

Correlations based on 1970 data from the World Bank's Social Data Bank are shown in table 2. The results for seven social indicators show a modest correlation with GNP (average $r^2 = 0.50$), while a sample of five economic indicators shows a somewhat higher correlation ($r^2 = 0.71$). When the social indicator data are disaggregated into samples of developing and developed countries, however, the correlation coefficients (technically, the square of the correlation coefficient is called the coefficient of determination) for both groups drop significantly ($r^2 = 0.25$ for developing countries, 0.18 for developed). Similar declines in the correlation are also found when the economic indicators are disaggregated. Apparently studies that examine only social variables for developing countries are apt to discover a poor relation with GNP, while those that consider economic and social variables for all countries are likely to find better relations.

One reason social indicators are not more highly correlated with GNP per head is that the relations are often distinctly nonlinear. Indicators such as life expectancy, literacy, and school enrollment have asymptotic limits that reflect biological and

14. Glen Sheehan and Michael Hopkins, *Basic Needs Performance: An Analysis of Some International Data,* World Employment Programme Research Working Paper, WEP 2-23/WP9 (Geneva: International Labour Office, 1978), p. 95.

15. See Wilfred Beckerman, *International Comparisons of Real Incomes* (Paris: OECD, 1966).

Table 2. *Correlation of Indicators with GNP per Head, 1970*

| Indicators | Coefficients of determination (r^2) | | | Sample size |
	All countries	Developing	Developed	
Social indicators				
Expectation of life at birth	0.53	0.28	0.13	102
Caloric consumption (as percentage of required)	0.44	0.22	0.02	103
Infant mortality	0.42	0.34	0.25	64
Primary enrollment	0.28	0.24	0.05	101
Literacy	0.54	0.47	0.16	70
Average persons per room (urban)	0.58	0.08	0.29	34
Housing units without piped water (percent)	0.74	0.13	0.36	36
Average	0.50	0.25	0.18	
Economic indicators per head				
Newsprint consumption	0.79	0.20	0.46	85
Automobiles	0.85	0.59	0.46	102
Radio receivers	0.43	0.14	0.07	97
Electricity consumption	0.67	0.30	0.24	102
Energy consumption	0.82	0.28	0.49	99
Average	0.71	0.30	0.34	

Note: This sample excludes the centrally planned economies and all countries with populations of less than 1 million. Although the total sample includes 106 countries, missing data reduce the sample size for each correlation.

Source: Based on data taken from the World Bank's Social Data Bank.

physical maximums. It is impossible, for instance, to have more than 100 percent literacy. These limits are often reached by middle-income countries, so that further increases in income show little gains in social indicators. For instance, life expectancy reaches seventy years of age for countries with income per head (1970) of $2,000, and it does not increase even as incomes increase to $5,000. Most countries have attained close to 100 percent literacy by the time their income per head reaches the $2,500 level. Conversely, countries below $500 GNP per head demonstrate a wide variety of social development that is largely unrelated to the level of GNP. This can be seen more clearly in figures 2 and 3. The cluster of points along both axes indicates the lack of

Figure 2. *GNP and Life Expectancy, 1970*

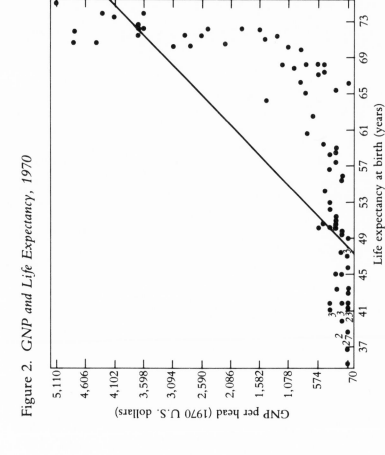

Note: Regression line: LE = 47.5 + 0.00689 GNP per head; R^2 = 0.53. Numbers in the graph indicate points with more than one observation.
Source: World Bank data.

Figure 3. *GNP and Literacy, 1970*

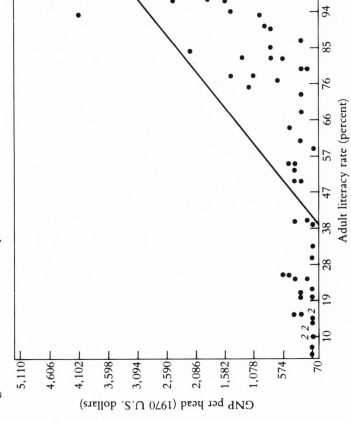

Note: Regression line: LIT = 42.15 + 0.0186 GNP per head; R^2 = 0.54. Numbers in the graph indicate points with more than one observation.
Source: World Bank data.

correlation between GNP and life expectancy and literacy at both the high- and low-income levels (other social indicators show similar patterns). It seems clear that a much better correlation could be developed by using some sort of nonlinear relation.[16] A nonlinear function would, however, obscure the fact that the correlation exists only among the middle-income countries. GNP per head is likely to be a misleading indicator of social development and progress in meeting basic needs, particularly when used in some linear fashion. Yet rankings of countries by social indicators and GNP are likely to be very similar because the ranking process obscures these nonlinearities.

Social Accounting Systems

Some work has been done on developing a system of social accounts to provide a kind of national accounting framework for social indicators. Stone and Seers have proposed the use of life-time activity sequences, calculated by dividing total life expectancy into segments.[17] Such tables would show the average time a person could expect to spend in various mutually exclusive states. One such matrix might divide lifetime activity between school, work, leisure, retirement, and the like, while another might be built on a marital sequence (single, married, divorced, widowed). Such tables would combine various important social statistics from different fields and would indicate changes over time, either actual or planned. But of the system's many problems, not the least is its inability to incorporate fully all aspects of social development. Some indicators (income distribution, security, police protection, pollution) cannot readily be transformed into segments of life expectancies. Furthermore, the system requires more data than are available in most countries and is thus more suited for those that are industrialized. Never-

---

16. For life expectancy, a semilog function increases the r^2 from 0.53 to 0.75

17. Richard Stone, *Toward a System of Social and Demographic Statistics* (New York: United Nations, 1975); and Dudley Seers, "Life Expectancy as an Integrating Concept in Social and Demographic Analysis and Planning," *Review of Income and Wealth,* ser. 23, no. 3 (September 1977), pp. 195-203.

theless, the concept has some potential for integrating a large variety of social variables and providing the basis for a theory linking policies to results in the area of social planning.

Other ideas have been developed for a more limited social accounting approach. The social accounting matrix (SAM) of Pyatt and Round does not utilize social indicators but expands the traditional input-output table into a matrix of payments made by productive sectors to different income recipients.[18] Recipients can be disaggregated in various ways to indicate the distribution of income between factors, urban and rural households, or income classes. The power of SAM is that it integrates production and income distribution data to give a better view of the economy and of the flows between sectors. It still relies, however, on the use of GNP as a measure of welfare and is limited in its application by the absence of good income distribution data.

Terleckyj has developed a matrix framework for analyzing the impact of government programs on various social goals, as indicated by the appropriate social indicators.[19] Since programs affect more than one social goal, the approach develops a matrix of inputs and outputs and suggests the possibility of defining the most efficient set of programs for achieving a particular set of goals. While this approach provides a useful rationale for using different indicators, it does not provide a better measure of growth or development.

Composite Indexes of Development

Relatively more work than has been done on a system of social accounts has gone into developing composite indexes to replace or supplement GNP as an indicator of social, economic, or general development. The U.N. Research Institute for Social Development (UNRISD) during the 1960s undertook to develop better

18. Graham Pyatt and Jeffrey Round, "Social Accounting Matrices for Development Planning," *Review of Income and Wealth,* ser. 23, no. 4 (December 1977), pp. 339-64.

19. Nestor Terleckyj, *Improvements in the Quality of Life* (Washington, D.C.: National Planning Association, 1975).

social indicators, including composite indicators. For instance, Drewnowski and Scott developed the Level of Living Index, which was defined as "the level of satisfaction of the needs of the population as measured by the flow of goods and services enjoyed in a unit of time."[20] The Level of Living Index itself, however, goes beyond the provision of goods and services and considers basic needs, subdivided between physical needs (nutrition, shelter, health) and cultural needs (education, leisure, security). "Higher needs" or "surplus over basic needs" is taken as the surplus income over some minimum level. The basic needs part of the index includes items that are very difficult to measure for many countries, such as the amount of leisure time available, the number of people in possession of private saving, and the quality of housing. This makes the index very difficult to apply, and Drewnowski and Scott were forced to use approximations even for their limited sample of twenty countries. Furthermore, the work, once begun, was not continued after 1966 in the same form.

McGranahan and others examined seventy-three indicators of economic and social characteristics and found a fairly high intercorrelation between them.[21] Through a process of elimination, they constructed the Development Index based on eighteen core indicators, which included nine social and nine economic indicators. The resulting index was highly correlated with GNP per head ($r^2 = 0.89$), although the ranking of some countries (Venezuela, Chile, and Japan) was substantially different under the index. In general, the correlation of the index and GNP per head was somewhat lower for developing than developed countries. McGranahan and others concluded that social development occurred at a more rapid pace than economic development up to a level of about $500 per head (1960 prices). Some of these results are themselves, however, a product of the method employed, since the eighteen core indicators were selected, in part, on the basis of their high intercorrelation with the other indicators. As a

20. Jan Drewnowski and Wolf Scott, "The Level of Living Index," Report no. 4 (Geneva: U.N. Research Institute for Social Development, 1966), p. 1.

21. McGranahan and others, *Contents and Measurement of Socio-Economic Development.*

result of the high intercorrelation, the composite index was relatively insensitive to the choice of component variables. McGranahan and others found, for instance, that the country rankings remained virtually unchanged when the number of indicators was reduced from eighteen to ten.

A study by the U.N. Economic and Social Council sought to analyze development by ranking 140 countries by seven indicators other than GNP.[22] These included two social indicators (literacy and life expectancy) and five economic indicators (energy, manufacturing share of GDP, manufacturing share of exports, employment outside agriculture, and number of telephones). An overall rank for each country was calculated by giving equal weight to the ranks under each separate indicator. When the results were arranged by quintiles and compared with GNP, the overall index was closely associated with the ranking by GNP. The U.N. index was heavily weighted by economic rather than purely social indicators, however, and thus tends to replicate the findings of Beckerman[23] and others that show nonmonetary indicators are highly correlated with GNP. A similar study by the OECD in 1973 used regression techniques for six variables to establish a predicted GNP per head index for eighty-two developing countries.[24] A 1977 paper by the OECD, however, concluded that "per capita GNP still appears to be the best measure" of the level of development.[25]

The use of a composite index has been studied by the Overseas Development Council (ODC), under the guidance of M. D. Morris.[26] Morris's Physical Quality of Life Index (PQLI) uses three simple indicators with equal weights to attempt to measure the fulfillment of "minimum human needs": life expectancy at

22. ECOSOC, "Developing Countries and Levels of Development."

23. Beckerman, *International Comparisons of Real Incomes.*

24. OECD, Development Assistance Committee, "Performance Compendium: Consolidated Results of Analytical Work on Economic and Social Performance of Developing Countries" (Paris, 1973).

25. OECD, Development Assistance Committee, "Socio-economic Typologies or Criteria and Their Usefulness in Measuring Development Progress."

26. M. D. Morris and F. B. Liser, "The PQLI: Measuring Progress in Meeting Human Needs," Communique on Development Issues no. 32 (Washington, D.C.: Overseas Development Council, 1977).

age one, infant mortality, and literacy. Morris argues that indicators used for judging performance under basic needs criteria should concentrate on outputs or results, rather than inputs. Input measures, he feels, do not measure success in meeting the desired goals and may lend an ethnocentric bias to the means employed. The use of only three indicators permits the calculation of the PQLI for a wide range of countries and facilitates the examination of changes in the index over time. The term "quality of life" is perhaps a misnomer, since what is really being measured is effectiveness in reducing mortality and raising literacy. Life expectancy measures the length, not the quality of life. (These ends also have an ethnocentric bias.) Most important, the weighting system of the PQLI is arbitrary, and there is no rationale for giving equal weights to literacy, infant mortality, and life expectancy at age one. It is not possible to prove that the PQLI gives a "correct" index of progress on human needs, as opposed to some alternative index having different weights or different components. It is not clear what is gained by combining the component indexes with a weighting system that cannot be defended. Analytical work can use the component indexes almost as easily as the composite index, without introducing the biases of the PQLI. While Morris's index, has received much attention in the popular press and has been incorporated in the 1979 report of the Development Assistance Committee of the OECD and in the World Almanac, most serious scholars find it difficult to accept the results of a composite index without a stronger theoretical foundation.

A similar but more complicated index has been constructed by Sivard for the U.S. Arms Control and Disarmament Agency.[27] She gives equal weight to three factors—GNP per head, education, and health—by averaging country ranks. Education and health indicators are themselves composed of an average of five factors each, combining input and output measures. The result is a ranking of countries according to combined economic and social performances that contains all the problems of other composite measures.

27. Ruth Sivard, "World Military and Social Expenditures, 1979" (Leesburg, Va.: World Priorities, 1979).

Despite the potential attractiveness of having a single index of socioeconomic development, there is little theoretical guidance to govern the choice of indicators, the correct scaling of component indexes, or the appropriate weights. Moreover, an index that relies only on ranking neglects the distance between ranks.

Scaling problems arise when raw data on social indicators are converted into component indexes ranging from 0 to 100. For instance, reasonable values for life expectancy could be either 40 to 75 years, or 40 to 100 years. A country with a life expectancy of 60 years will obviously have a different "score" depending on the scaling chosen (57 as opposed to 33; that is, 20 years' superiority expressed as a proportion of the interval 35 or 60 and multiplied by 100), and this will materially change the composite index. Furthermore, the scaling system need not be linear. Drewnowski used "expert opinion" to derive a linear scale system reflecting set levels of basic needs satisfaction. McGranahan and others developed an elaborate system of correspondence points to determine the appropriate scale range and utilized nonlinear (logarithmic) scaling for many indicators. Morris simply took the range of the data for each indicator, with the "worst" country being defined as 0 and the "best" as 100.

An even more difficult problem concerns the proper weights to be used in combining the component indexes into the composite. Drewnowski tried both equal fixed weights and a system of sliding weights under which deviations from the normal were given more weight than indexes close to the normal. The rankings of countries by sliding or equal weights were highly correlated with the rankings of countries by GNP per head or consumption per head, and the shift in the weighting system did not materially affect the rankings. McGranahan's weighting system gave greater weight to the component indicators that had the highest degree of intercorrelation with the other indicators, a somewhat dubious method. The absence of correlation might be thought an equally valid criterion, though it might then be asked why there is no correlation and why the indicators should be integrated. McGranahan also found that moderate changes in the weighting system did not affect the level of each country's index or its ranking. The insensitivity of the general index to the choice of weights is a logical result of having high intercorrelation among the components, since the high correlation implies that any one component is a good substitute for any other. The U.N. ECOSOC study gives equal weight to the country *ranks* of the social indicators, thus avoiding, in a certain sense, the scaling problem. As mentioned above, the PQLI gives equal weight to each of the three components without ascertaining if this implies the correct tradeoff between the various components. None of these studies indicates that much effort was devoted to developing a theoretically sound rationale for the weighting system. If one is ever found, it will have to be based on the relative preferences of people.

Because of these problems, it might well be argued that a composite index is either unnecessary, or undesirable, or impossible to construct. It is unnecessary if the components are highly correlated with one another, because then any one of the component indicators by itself will serve as an adequate index. If, however, the components move in different directions in cross-country comparisons and time series, averaging would conceal the important issues and would be undesirable. Using the same index for a situation in which mortality is high and literacy low, as for one in which literacy is high and mortality low, implies evaluating the tradeoff between literacy and life expectancy. Unless the basis for such an evaluation can be established, all weighting remains arbitrary and misleading, and composition is impossible. The case for considering the two indexes separately is exactly the same as the case for having an index independent of GNP.

If basic needs were interpreted literally, all needs that were "basic" would have to be met together, and tradeoffs between different basic needs would be ruled out. A composite index would therefore not be necessary. As long as the package of basic needs has not been fully met, no amount of additional satisfaction of any one component could compensate for the slightest deficiency in any other, so that a composite indicator would be ruled out. Once all basic needs had been met, again no composite index would be required, for the indicator for any one need would show that all had been satisfied. But I am not advocating such a literal interpretation of basic needs.

Conclusions

This brief survey has reviewed four alternatives to GNP per head for calculating some of the dimensions of development. The adjustment-to-GNP approach has focused largely on improving GNP as a measure of economic welfare. Attempts to introduce other costs and benefits of development, which would make GNP a broader measure of welfare, lack a logical basis and tend instead to result in a confusion of concepts. Research on social indicators has failed to produce an alternative that is as readily accepted and comprehended as GNP per head, though such indicators are useful for judging social performance. Systems of social accounts, which could integrate social indicators through some unifying concept, have not been able to overcome successfully all the difficult problems encountered.

Efforts to develop composite indexes have ranged from a search for better measures of the physical production of goods and services to a measure of the quality of life, of economic or social welfare, of satisfactions, happiness, and other objectives. The search for a composite index of social welfare, analogous to GNP as an index of production, has been fruitless so far, since it has proven virtually impossible to translate every aspect of social progress into monetary values or some other readily accepted common denominator. The great deal of work devoted to composite indexes, however, suggests the need for a single number which, like GNP per head, can be quickly grasped as a rough indication of social development.

The current discussion of basic needs–oriented development focuses on the alleviation of poverty through a variety of measures other than merely the redistribution of incremental output. Attention to *how much* is being produced is supplemented by attention to *what* is being produced, how, for whom, and with what impact. Obviously, the rapid growth of output will still be important to the alleviation of poverty, and GNP per head remains an important figure. What is required in addition are some indicators of the composition and beneficiaries of GNP and of the results of output growth—indicators that would supplement the

GNP data, not replace them. The basic needs approach, therefore, can give the necessary focus to work on social indicators.

As a first step, it might be useful to define the best indicator for each of the essential basic needs, at present considered to be in six areas: nutrition, primary education, health, sanitation, water supply, and housing and related infrastructure.[28] This list is merely illustrative, not exhaustive, and all needs do not have the same status. A limited set of core indicators covering these areas would be a useful device for concentrating efforts to collect more adequate, standardized, comparable international statistics on basic needs. From the fact that we consider six basic needs, it does not necessarily follow that there be six core indicators. More than one indicator may be necessary to measure adequately progress in any one area, or one indicator may serve more than one basic needs sector. Nevertheless, the basic needs concept can serve to integrate efforts to gather and analyze data.

Once defined, these core basic needs indicators could be important in policy analysis, permitting, for instance, international comparisons of performance and of relative aid levels. Such indicators could be used to view the relative gap between rich and poor countries and the speed with which this gap is widening or narrowing. They would indicate which countries are meeting the basic needs of their citizens and how their policies are related to the growth of output, trade, investment, and so on.

Because work on social indicators has often lacked a sharp focus, a large number of disparate indicators have been collected and tabulated. It might be more fruitful to concentrate work on a few important indicators and to improve their quality and coverage. In particular, it would be useful to add a distributional dimension to indicators now collected as averages. Instead of, for example, average caloric consumption, it would be preferable to compare caloric consumption of the highest income quartile with that of the lowest. The same goes for life expectancy, literacy, infant mortality, school enrollment, and so on. Similarly, distinct figures for males and females would reveal a great

28. Paul Streeten and Shahid Javed Burki, "Basic Needs: Some Issues," *World Development,* vol. 6, no. 3 (March 1978), pp. 411-21.

deal about the distribution of the goods and services that meet basic needs.

Selection of the appropriate index in each field is best left to technical experts in each sector, but the following list suggests indicators that might be included:

Basic need	*Indicator*
Health	Life expectancy at birth
Education	Literacy Primary school enrollment as a percentage of the population aged five to fourteen
Food	Calorie supply per head or calorie supply as a percentage of requirements
Water supply	Infant mortality per thousand births Percentage of population with access to potable water
Sanitation	Infant mortality per thousand births Percentage of population with access to sanitation facilities

This identification of core indicators follows the philosophy of this chapter by stressing measures of results, rather than inputs. In accordance with the conclusion of the U.N. Research Institute for Social Development, infant mortality is assumed to be a good indicator of the availability of sanitation and clean water facilities; as a supplementary indicator, input measures have also been identified. While literacy is a good general measure of progress in education, the percentage of the relevant age group enrolled in primary school is included to measure country effort. It has not been possible, however, to identify a satisfactory measure of housing needs. The only readily available indicator is people per room, but this is merely a rough index of crowding and does not convey much about the quality of housing.

If an acceptable system of weights could be developed, it might be possible to combine the core indicators into a composite basic needs index. The chances of doing so are, however, extremely small. Despite considerable research on composite indexes, no one has come close to developing a rational weighting system. Critics might question the desirability of such a composite index, even if it could be constructed, because it would conceal the basis for important choices.

Instead of attempting to develop a composite index of basic needs, a useful alternative might be to narrow the range of indicators from six to one or two, which correlate highly with basic needs fulfillment. This approach would serve the needs of those who desire a single number for making quick judgments on social performance, without introducing the problems of weighted composite indexes. The prospects for doing this are considerably enhanced because many so-called basic needs in fact refer to inputs rather than to ultimate goals. Certainly nutrition, water supply, and sanitation are valued because they improve the health of the population; to a more limited extent, this is also true of housing and education. All can be considered inputs into the health "production function." Although they may be valued for other reasons, their influence on health accounts for the close association of the individual core indicators with the others. Therefore, it could be argued that some measure of health, such as life expectancy at birth, would be a good single measure of basic needs.

In a sense, life expectancy is a kind of weighted "composite" of progress in meeting physiological basic needs. It has the advantage of capturing the impact on individuals, not only of nonmarket factors but also of income net of taxes, transfer payments, and social services, without raising all the difficulties of income measures. These difficulties include identifying the appropriate unit (individual, household, or family), the appropriate magnitude (capital, consumption, or income), and the appropriate set of prices (market prices or international prices) and determining what to value as final goods and what as costs. As a basic needs indicator, life expectancy might be regarded as superior not only to a composite index of social indicators but also to GNP and to indexes of income distribution. It is possible for two countries to register the same GNP per head and the same ratio of income accruing to the poorest 20 percent, and yet to have different average life expectancies. For some purposes—for example, to distinguish between meeting the basic needs of men and women or of rural and urban populations, or to acquire additional information if life expectancies cluster very near one another—it would be useful to add a measure of progress in education, such as literacy. It is, of course, possible to have a long and miserable life, and one might wish to put an upper limit to the desired life span. Thomas Hobbes said that in the state of nature a human life was nasty, brutish, and short. In the early stages of development it has become nasty, brutish, and long. It is true that at low income levels there is a higher correlation between morbidity and mortality than at higher income levels, and for this reason life expectancy covers some dimensions of health as well as the length of life. But it does not do this perfectly, and it would be desirable to have indicators of the true quality, as well the quantity, of life.

In using a single indicator, it is, however, important to guard against the danger of interpreting either the result or the inputs in a unidimensional way. Policies to increase life expectancy can affect different age groups differently: improved nutrition, for example, may affect life expectancy above one year, whereas women's education may affect infant mortality. Furthermore, the improvement of a single indicator such as life expectancy will divert attention to health measures generally and doctors, clinics, and nurses specifically, whereas the production function for life expectancy may include a number of thrusts to improve jobs, earnings, and environments, which are not obviously related to health. Just as reductions in the rate of population growth are not simply a function of improved family planning, so improved health and longer life are not simply a function of improved health delivery systems. But as long as the indicators are not identified with unidimensional results or unicausal remedies, there is much to be said for a simple system of recording and monitoring.

4

Basic Needs and Growth: Is There a Conflict?

CRITICS OF THE BASIC NEEDS APPROACH have often stated that it sacrifices savings, productive investment, and incentives to work for the sake of current consumption and welfare. Although the problem is usually presented as a tradeoff between basic needs and growth, the two objectives are not strictly comparable. If the main goal is growth, the emphasis is on annual increments of production and income and concern for the future. A basic needs approach must also contain a time dimension and propose policies that increasingly meet a dynamic range of the basic needs of a growing population.

If basic needs and growth are to be compared at all, the question should be: Does meeting basic needs now imply sacrificing certain components of current output or certain components of current incomes? Such a sacrifice may reduce aggregate growth of income per head by raising the capital-output ratio, lowering the savings ratio, or raising population growth—or by any combination of the three. Analysis of the relation between basic needs and growth raises additional questions. First, how does the *process* of reaching the state when basic needs are met affect growth? Second, after basic needs are met how does this *achievement* affect subsequent economic growth? Third, how does the rate and pattern of growth in turn affect the willingness and capacity to meet basic needs?

Four types of tradeoff can be envisaged: (1) between the consumption of higher income groups and benefits to lower income groups; (2) between non–basic needs goods and services consumed by *all* income groups, including the poor, and basic needs goods and services consumed only by the poor; (3) between activities that create incentives for larger savings and efforts to work, and current consumption; (4) between goods and services that make a larger contribution to future production and those that make a smaller contribution or none. All these tradeoffs have certain distributional dimensions, in both space and time; they imply decisions about how goods and services are distributed. Those who suspect that a basic needs approach involves a tradeoff with growth are concerned that succeeding generations would have to accept lower levels of living than if the present generation were asked to tighten its belt now for greater prosperity later.

Whether resources to meet basic needs are diverted from non–basic needs consumption or physical investment depends on the circumstances of the particular country. The two issues at stake are: Does meeting basic needs reduce productive investments; and does meeting basic needs itself contribute to growth?

The high spenders on basic needs, Cuba and Sri Lanka, had roughly average investment ratios, while the low spenders, Indonesia and Brazil, had above average investment ratios. But the low spenders spent more than the average ratio of income on non–basic needs consumption. Taiwan, South Korea, the Philippines, Paraguay, and Thailand do well on basic needs and have above average investment ratios, while Sri Lanka, Cuba, Jamaica, Colombia, and Uruguay, also good basic needs performers, have average investment ratios. There is no evidence that a basis needs approach is systematically associated with low investment ratios.

It is even more difficult to assess whether policies to meet basic needs lower growth by raising capital-output ratios. This issue is a large umbrella that covers the impact of basic needs policies on incentives to innovate and manage enterprises, for which some non–basic needs goods are necessary, on the degree of capital utilization, and on the pattern of investment. There is no evidence that a basic needs approach necessarily reduces the productivity of whatever investment is done. On theoretical grounds, one would expect that it would raise productivity. The most

Figure 4. *Relation between Economic Growth and Improvement in Meeting Basic Needs*

	Economic growth +	
Brazil		*Taiwan* *South Korea* *Sri Lanka (1960–70)* *Indonesia (1970–76)*
		Change in basic needs indicators
−		+
Mali *Indonesia (1960–70)*		*Somalia* *Sri Lanka (1970–76)* *Cuba* *Egypt*
	−	

+ Above average for group.
− Below average for group.

Source: John C. H. Fei, Gustav Ranis, and Frances Stewart, "Basic Needs: A Framework for Analysis" (Washington, D.C.: World Bank, April 1979; processed).

important qualification is the need for incentives, which require non–basic needs goods and services and a degree of inequality.

Figure 4 relates above average and below average economic growth and performance in meeting basic needs (as reflected by basic needs indicators and their improvement) for different countries. The sample of seven economies examined in the work of the World Bank (Brazil, Cuba, Egypt, Indonesia, Mali, Somalia, and Sri Lanka) has a disproportionately large number of slow growers, as the figure illustrates. For the sake of completeness, I have added the examples of Taiwan and South Korea to show that any combination of growth and change in basic needs indicators is possible.

Brazil has a growth rate that is well above the average and a change in indicators below average. Its high investment rate was partly at the expense of public consumption. Between 1960 and 1976 public consumption as a share of GDP fell by 2 percent in Brazil, while the investment ratio rose by 5 percent. Moreover, the pattern of growth was disproportionately concentrated on non–basic needs consumption goods—as indicated by the heavy expenditure on consumer durables among quite low-income groups. In contrast, in Taiwan and South Korea above average improvements in basic needs indicators accompanied above average growth rates—a trend supporting the view that it is the pattern rather than the rate of growth which determines the impact on basic needs. In both cases the share of public consumption fell during the period, while the investment rate rose. This pattern indicates that the level of public consumption as a share of GDP is not critical to meeting basic needs. Sri Lanka also showed above average growth (particularly for a South Asian country) and above average improvement in basic needs for 1960–70, although its growth was not as spectacular as that of South Korea and Taiwan. It was suggested earlier that there may be many routes to the satisfaction of basic needs; this possibility is supported by the variety of experience shown here. Others could easily be added.

As figure 4 illustrates, high rates of economic growth are neither necessary nor sufficient to generate improvements in basic needs. While the high spenders in this small sample are concentrated in the below average growth category, the experience of Sri Lanka between 1960 and 1970 suggests it is possible to combine public expenditure on basic needs with respectable growth.

If problems of measurement are ignored for the moment, the various options can be represented by four paths to increasing the consumption of the poor. In figure 5 the log of consumption per head of the poor is traced on the vertical axis, and time on the horizontal axis. Path 1 first shows lower levels of consumption but, as a result of better incentives and productive investment, overtakes path 2 at some point (T_1) and, for ever after, the consumption of the poor is higher. Path 2 starts with higher consumption by the poor but, by neglecting incentives, private and public savings, and productive investment, falls behind path 1 after a certain date, T_1. This is how the option is often presented. (It should be clear that sound policies would rule out path 3, which is an inefficient way of meeting the needs of the poor.) The rationale behind basic needs, however, is path 4. High priority is given to some components of current consumption by

Figure 5. *Comparison of the Effects over Time of Four Approaches to Increasing Consumption by the Poor*

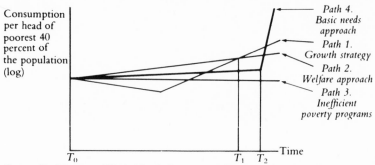

Source: Paul Streeten, "Basic Needs: Premises and Promises," *Journal of Policy Modeling,* vol. 1 (1979), pp. 136–46.

the poor, which may for a while fall below the consumption levels that could have been attained by the two other efficient paths. When the present generation of children enters the labor force and begins to yield returns (T_2), growth is steeper than it would have been under path 1; it overtakes first the welfare path 2 and later the growth path 1. The *process* of meeting basic needs may reduce growth insofar as resources are diverted from investment to consumption, but the *achievement* of massive investment in human capital will speed up growth because human capital has become more productive.

Stalinist-forced industrialization and the Industrial Revolution in England followed path 1. Taiwan, Korea, and perhaps Japan followed path 4, laying in early years the runway for a future "takeoff into self-sustained growth" (the phrase is W. W. Rostow's) by meeting certain basic needs through land reform and massive investment in human capital, especially education. Critics charge that Sri Lanka and Tanzania may be following path 2 and Burma path 3, though these experiences have not yet been fully analyzed.[1]

---

1. Paul Isenman in his article, "Basic Needs: The Case of Sri Lanka," *World Development,* vol. 8, no. 3 (March 1980), pp. 237-58, suggests that meeting basic needs in Sri

Some tentative econometric work has tended to be consistent with the hypothesis put forward here.[2] Various indicators of the extent to which basic needs were met in 1960 were related to GNP growth rates between 1960 and 1973 for eighty-three economies and the twelve with the highest growth. It was found that substantial progress in meeting basic needs does not subsequently lead to lower growth rates; that better performance in meeting basic needs tends to lead to higher growth rates in the future; and that improved health, as reflected in longer life expectancy, is as strongly related to growth as is educational attainment measured by literacy, though education affects growth by improving not only production skills but also living skills and, therefore, hygiene and health.

A simple way of testing the relation between basic needs and growth is to compare the basic needs performance of some rapidly growing economies with that of the average. Table 3 shows the relation between life expectancy, literacy, and growth in the twelve fastest growing economies between 1960 and 1977 (excluding oil exporters and those with populations of less than 1 million) compared with the average developing country. The average annual growth rate of the rapid growers, 5.7 percent, was substantially higher than the average for the whole sample, 2.4 percent. The average life expectancy in these rapidly growing economies was 61 years at the beginning of the period in 1960, compared with 48 for the average. Literacy was also much higher. It may be concluded that good performance in meeting basic needs accelerates, or at least does not retard, growth.

Lanka did not retard growth. Ajit Singh and Manfred Bienefeld suggest a similar conclusion in the case of Tanzania in "Industry and Urban Economy in Tanzania," background paper for the ILO, Jobs and Skills Programme for Africa, Employment Advisory Mission to Tanzania (Addis Ababa, circa 1977; processed).

2. Norman L. Hicks, "Growth versus Basic Needs: Is There a Trade-off?" *World Development,* vol. 7, no. 11/12 (November/December 1979), pp. 985-94; and "Is There a Trade-off between Growth and Basic Needs?" *Finance & Development,* vol. 17, no. 2 (June 1980), pp. 17-20. See also David Morawetz, "Basic Needs Policies and Population Growth," *World Development,* vol. 6, no. 11/12 (November/December 1978), pp. 1251-59; and David Wheeler, "Basic Needs Fulfillment and Economic Growth: A Simultaneous Model," *Journal of Development Economics,* vol. 7, no. 4 (December 1980), pp. 435-51.

Table 3. *Economic Growth, Life Expectancy, and Literacy in Selected Economies*

Economy	Growth rate, 1960–77[a] (percent)	Life expectancy, 1960 (years)	Deviation from expected level of life expectancy[b] (years)	Adult literacy, 1960 (percent)	Deviation from expected level of literacy, 1960[c] (percent)
Singapore	7.7	64.0	3.1	—	—
Korea	7.6	54.0	11.1	71.0	43.6
Taiwan	6.5	64.0	15.5	54.0	14.2
Hong Kong	6.3	65.0	6.5	70.0	6.4
Greece	6.1	68.0	5.7	81.0	7.5
Portugal	5.7	62.0	4.7	62.0	1.7
Spain	5.3	68.0	1.8	87.0	1.2
Yugoslavia	5.2	62.0	4.7	77.0	16.7
Brazil	4.9	57.0	3.0	61.0	8.6
Israel	4.6	69.0	2.0	—	—
Thailand	4.5	51.0	9.5	68.0	43.5
Tunisia	4.3	48.0	-0.5	16.0	-23.8
Average of 12 economies	5.7	61.0	5.6	64.7	12.0
Average of total sample[d]	2.4	48.0	-0.0	37.6	-0.0

— Not available.

a. Growth rate of real GNP per head.

b. Deviations from estimated values derived from an equation where life expectancy (*LE*) in 1960 is related to income per head (*Y*) in 1960 in the following way: $LE = 34.29 + 0.07679 \, Y - 0.000043 \, Y^2$ ($r^2 = 0.66$).

c. Deviations from estimated values derived from an equation where literacy (*LIT*) in 1960 is related to income per head (*Y*) in 1967 in the following way: $LIT = 9.23 + 0.1595 \, Y - 0.0000658 \, Y^2$ ($r^2 = 0.44$).

d. Data for average growth rates and life expectancy refer to a sample of 83 countries, while those for literacy cover 63 countries.

Source: Data from World Bank, *World Development Report, 1979* (New York: Oxford University Press, 1979); table from Norman Hicks, "Is There a Trade-off between Growth and Basic Needs?" *Finance & Development*, vol. 17, no. 2 (June 1980), pp. 19 and 20.

But the data presented in the table have a bias. The twelve fastest growing economies had incomes higher than the average in 1960. Since income and life expectancy are associated, it is not surprising to find that the rapid growers showed higher life expectancy. To remove this bias Norman Hicks calculated an equation relating life expectancy to income and thereby established the "expected" life expectancy for every country. Better than normal life expectancy can then be measured by the deviation of the actual from the expected level. These deviations are shown in the third column of table 3. The twelve fast growing economies show life expectancies that are on average 5.1 years higher than their expected figure. Of the difference of 13 years (61 − 48) between the average for the twelve economies and that for the sample of eighty-three, about 8 years are due to differences in income and 5 to other factors.

Norman Hicks did the same exercise for literacy. In the twelve rapidly growing economies about 65 percent of the adults were literate in 1960, compared with 38 percent for the entire sample. When adjusted for differences in income levels, literacy rates in the fast growers were about 13 percent above those in the other economies at the beginning of the period.

In table 4 the question is turned around to ask how the best performers in meeting basic needs (those with the largest deviation from expected levels of life expectancy) have performed with respect to growth. Many of the same names appear on this list, such as Taiwan, South Korea, Thailand, Hong Kong, and Greece. But others, such as Sri Lanka, Paraguay, the Philippines, Burma, and Kenya, have done well on life expectancy without registering spectacularly high growth rates (an average of about 2 percent) between 1960 and 1977. Nevertheless, the average annual growth rate of 4 percent for this group of good basic needs performers is considerably higher than the average for the whole group of 2.4 percent. Clearly, many factors other than good basic needs performance are responsible for growth: investment, capital flows, exports, macroeconomic policies, cultural factors, and so on. And statistical correlations between basic needs fulfillment and growth rates cannot identify which is cause and which effect. The causal link would be expected to

Table 4. *Growth and Life Expectancy in Selected Economies*

Economy	Deviation from expected level of life expectancy (years)	Growth rate, 1960–77 (percent)
Sri Lanka	22.5	1.9
Taiwan	15.5	6.5
Korea	11.1	7.6
Thailand	9.5	4.5
Malaysia	7.3	4.0
Paraguay	6.9	2.4
Philippines	6.8	2.1
Hong Kong	6.5	6.3
Panama	6.1	3.7
Burma	6.0	0.9
Greece	5.7	6.1
Kenya	5.5	2.4
Average of 12 economies	9.1	4.0
Average of 83 economies	0	2.4

Note: For explanation of variables, see table 3.
Source: Same as table 3.

work both ways: from basic needs to growth, and from growth to basic needs. But the sequence of events in table 3, showing literacy rates and life expectancy in 1960 and growth rates in 1960-77, suggests strongly that good basic needs performance contributes to good growth. If these econometric exercises are taken together with microeconomic studies of specific projects, the indication is that, far from retarding growth, the right kind of basic needs performance can be an important contribution to it.

The hypothesis that good basic needs performance contributes to faster growth hinges on the assumption that meeting basic needs is also an investment in human capital, and that in time this investment yields higher rates of return than do alternative investments. It is fairly obvious that some forms of investment in human capital, like some forms of physical investment, can be wasted and not contribute to national productivity. Educated and healthy people may migrate abroad and contribute to growth in other countries. Aspirations aroused by education may lead to wage or job demands that deter industrial development and swell the ranks of the educated unemployed. The content of health services and education and the people served will vary according to whether policies are guided primarily by basic needs or productivity. It is equally evident from a comparison of the tables that the investment in human capital has to be complemented by appropriate policies in other areas, such as physical investment, export earnings, and foreign capital flows.

A growing body of evidence indicates that meeting basic needs in the correct policy context can be a powerful method of improving the quality of human resources. A healthy and well-fed labor force is capable of greater physical and mental effort than one that is ill, hungry, and malnourished. A whole range of skills acquired through education and training is essential for the production of many goods and services. Widespread education also facilitates communication and thereby mobilizes a greater pool of talent. It makes people more flexible and helps them adapt to the changes brought by economic growth. Several studies suggest a strong link between education and labor productivity. A direct relation between primary education and the productivity of labor and capital has been demonstrated both in agriculture in several developing countries and in the Japanese cotton-spinning industry from 1891 to 1935. It is probable that the outstanding growth performance of Japan, South Korea, Taiwan, and Israel is largely due to the high levels of literacy and numeracy attained in these countries at an early stage of development.[3]

When comparing growth paths, it is important to measure growth and its components correctly. Basic needs are measured in terms of physiological needs and physical inputs, and financial costs are calculated from these. Growth, however, is an aggregate in which the existing, often very unequal, income distribution determines purchasing power and, with it, the price

---

3. For a fuller discussion and references to the evidence of the productive aspects of satisfying basic needs, see World Bank, *World Development Report, 1980* (New York: Oxford University Press, 1980), especially chaps. 4 and 5.

weights. A 10 percent increase in the income of someone earning $10,000 is weighted a hundred times that of a 10 percent increase in the income of someone earning $100. Ahluwalia and Chenery have suggested a modification of the conventional growth measure: the initial shares of each income group are weighted by their share in the national income, so that the weight of the poorest is the smallest and that of the richest, the largest.[4] One possibility is to weight each group equally, according to the number of people (or households, allowing for size and age distribution), so that a 1 percent growth of the income of the poorest 25 percent has the same weight as a 1 percent growth of that of the richest 25 percent. An even more radical system of weighting would attribute zero weights to the growth of income of all income groups above the poorest 25 or 40 percent, and a weight of unity to those below the poverty line. Whichever method is chosen, any discussion of the tradeoff between basic needs and growth ought to specify the weights attached to income growth of different income groups. This would bring out clearly the value judgments underlying the strategy.

The relative importance of different items in the consumption basket is normally determined by their relative prices. Growth is registered when the consumption of whiskey has risen, even though the consumption of milk may have declined. This is not because whiskey consumed by the rich is regarded as more important than milk consumed by the poor, but because the higher incomes of the rich determine the relatively high price of whiskey, while lack of purchasing power of the poor is reflected in the low price of milk. In societies with unequal income distribution, the standard measure for GNP growth therefore gives excessive weight to the growth of non–basic needs goods and deficient weight to basic needs goods.

When the particular resources needed for the particular vulnerable groups have been specified and a time profile defined for meeting the basic needs of a growing population on a sustainable

---

4. Montek S. Ahluwalia and Hollis Chenery, "A Model of Distribution and Growth," in Hollis Chenery and others, *Redistribution with Growth* (London: Oxford University Press, 1974), pp. 209–35.

basis, growth will turn out to be the *result* of a basic needs policy, not its objective. Growth is not normally something that has to be sacrificed or traded off to meet present needs. On the contrary, in the light of the above considerations, a basic needs approach may well call for higher growth rates than a so-called growth strategy. But the time path, the composition, the beneficiaries, and the measure of such growth will be different from those of a conventional high-growth strategy.

This raises the third question posed at the beginning of this chapter: How does economic growth affect the provision for basic needs? A higher rate of growth increases the resources available for meeting basic needs. A large component of the goods that minister to basic needs is produced and sold in the private sector in many countries, especially food, shelter, household goods, transport, energy, and clothes. The ability of the poor to raise their consumption of these basic goods depends on the growth of their incomes and the availability and prices of these goods. In countries where rapid growth is not accompanied by an adequate rate of growth of incomes of the poor, their basic needs may not be met as speedily as they are in more slowly growing countries with higher rates of growth of the incomes of the poor.

The concern here is with real incomes, not money incomes. In countries such as Brazil and Indonesia that register high growth rates, it appears that the prices of staple foods have tended to rise more than the average price level, so that the incomes of the poor have suffered. In a basic needs approach it is important to stabilize basic food prices for the urban poor, the landless laborers, and food deficit farmers who have to buy food, without discouraging food production by poor farmers. If the low incomes of the poor are eroded by purchases of expensive nutrients and non–basic needs goods, the high prices further reduce the impact of growth on the satisfaction of basic needs.

Public services provided free, such as education, still require out-of-pocket expenditure on books, clothes, and transport. The use of these free services also imposes costs in the form of relinquished earnings when, for example, children attend school or patients go to a hospital. Thus a rise in personal income is a condition for securing access to publicly provided free services. High growth rates enable public expenditure to rise, but again much depends upon the allocation of public expenditure both among sectors (whether it goes for defense or education) and within each sector (for tertiary or primary education). Public expenditure often reinforces the biases in the private sector that favor towns over country, richer regions over poorer regions, and the middle class over the poor.

Growth by itself—even egalitarian growth or redistribution from growth—does not guarantee the satisfaction of basic needs. A distinctive feature of the basic needs approach is that policies must be implemented to ensure a rising and properly distributed supply of goods, both private and public, if basic needs are to be met.

5

Lessons from
Country Experience

A BASIC NEEDS APPROACH TO DEVELOPMENT tries to ensure that all human beings have the opportunity to live full lives. The approach (on the broader of the two definitions discussed in the section "The Basic Needs Approach" in chapter 1) has three objectives:

—Real incomes that are adequate to buy necessities such as food, clothing, household goods, transport, fuel, and shelter. This in turn implies productive and remunerative livelihoods (employment and self-employment) that give people a primary claim to what they produce and recognition of their contribution.
—Access to public services such as education, health care, water, and sanitation. This implies a physical and social infrastructure adequate to provide basic goods and services on a sustained basis and to allow for the growing fulfillment of basic needs.
—Participation in the formulation and implementation of projects, programs, and policies by the people affected and local mobilization of underutilized resources.

To conventional efforts to eradicate poverty by increasing incomes, consumption, and employment (including self-employment), the basic needs approach as narrowly defined adds another dimension: provision of the particular goods and services needed by deprived groups—those who starve or are malnourished, those who are suffering from ill health, the homeless, the illiterate. In measuring development performance it is necessary to adjust money income for price changes to arrive at real income, and to add to measures of average income others that get at its distribution. Similarly, in the basic needs approach it is necessary to probe behind real income and its distribution to get at the goods and services (such as food) the income buys, to probe behind these goods and services to get at their characteristics (such as calories), and to probe behind these characteristics to get at the human needs they meet (such as nutrition and health). The focus of the World Bank's recent work has been on achieving adequate standards of health and education by securing access to a range of goods and services that would remove hunger and malnutrition, disease, illiteracy, and lack of safe water, sanitation, and decent shelter.

How is the objective of meeting basic needs translated into action? For operational purposes there are three aspects of the approach: supply, demand, and institutions. There must be adequate production (including distribution and foreign trade) of the goods in question, there must be adequate purchasing power by the poor to buy them, and the organizational arrangements must facilitate access and delivery in both the market and the nonmarket sectors. The type of institutional arrangements determines the costs and effectiveness of meeting basic needs.

The pattern of production must conform to the demand for basic goods and services; otherwise rising prices of the necessities demanded or falling prices of the goods produced and sold by the poor will frustrate the policies intended to improve their lot. Production must cover not only currently required basic goods (and exports to pay for imported basic goods), but also investment goods to provide for the future satisfaction of basic needs.

On the side of demand, primary, secondary, and tertiary demand must be distinguished. Primary demand is created by increasing the earning power of the poor through employment or the ownership of assets such as land. Secondary demand is created by channeling public services such as education and training to the poor, so that their productivity and earning power increase. Tertiary demand is created by transfer payments to the poor either in cash or in kind. The three areas overlap; for example, transfer payments may improve earning power by making people healthier.

The institutional framework has tended to be neglected in many conventional approaches. In the basic needs approach, it is, however, of crucial importance. Basic needs are met by the market when people use their income to buy essential goods; they are met by the public sector through free services and transfers of income; they are met by community action, by cooperative and voluntary organizations; and they are met in households. The activities of the household are particularly relevant to the basic needs approach. The household allocates the wage incomes earned by its members, and it produces goods and services for its own use. Although its own production may account for as much as 40 percent of household income in developing countries, it forms a much larger proportion of income and production in the basic needs sectors. Moreover, household activities play a crucial role in converting education, health, nutrition, and the like into improvements in the quality of individual lives.[1]

The public sector is also important in a basic needs approach as a producer, a maker of rules, and a source of finance. Transfer payments and subsidies are paid out of public revenues, and the government makes and enforces the laws to which private transactions are subject. Health services, education, and sanitation facilities are commonly concentrated in the public sector. One reason the basic needs approach is necessary is that the previous emphasis on minimum incomes and poverty lines tended to neglect the household and the public sector, both of which figure prominently in the provision of basic needs goods and services. Analysis of the public sector must cover administrative and political arrangements to determine the best combination of local responsibility and central support and the administrative structure most appropriate for meeting basic needs.

A basic needs approach must combine emphases on the supply of basic goods, the demand for basic goods, and the appropriate

1. In "A Branch of Economics Is Missing: Micro-Micro Theory," *Journal of Economic Literature*, vol. 17, no. 2 (June 1979), pp. 477-502, Harvey Leibenstein pleads for more analysis of intrafirm behavior. The same arguments apply to intrahousehold behavior.

institutional arrangements for matching supply with needs. Failure in any of these areas can lead to a failure in meeting basic needs. Different parts of this book stress different aspects, according to the context.

An effective basic needs program calls for action on five distinct levels, at each of which supply, demand, and institutions are relevant.

—The most direct and speediest intervention is to deliver basic goods or the money to buy them to the poor, but it is expensive and may be not only incapable of being sustained, but also ineffective unless supported by action on the other three levels.

—Sectoral intervention is necessary to improve the access of the poor to basic goods and services, such as health, education, or food.

—Macroeconomic policies that affect the rate of growth, employment creation, incomes, and prices are necessary to prevent the nonpoor from capturing the gains from improvement in human capital and the consequential gains in productivity.

—Structural changes relating to the system of landownership and tenancy laws, to the ownership of other assets, and to population policies may be needed to put the satisfaction of basic needs on a sustainable basis and allow for increases in the goods and services provided.

—International assistance is needed, particularly in the case of the poorest countries, to support and supplement domestic efforts. The time dimension of intervention is, of course, different at each level. In some cases action on one or two levels may be enough to set up linkages with other levels through incentives and market forces. In others, simultaneous intervention on several or all levels is needed.

Country Experience

Although development experience spans only three decades since World War II, developing countries exhibit a very wide range of experience in meeting the basic needs of their people.[2] If literacy rates and life expectancy are used as rough measures of basic needs performance, life expectancy in 1977 was estimated to be less than forty-five years in twelve countries (with populations of more than half a million)—Afghanistan, Angola, Bhutan, Chad, Ethiopia, Guinea, Lao People's Democratic Republic, Mali, Mauritania, Niger, Senegal, and Somalia. It was seventy years or more in ten developing economies—Argentina, Costa Rica, Cuba, Hong Kong, Jamaica, Panama, Singapore, Taiwan, Trinidad and Tobago, and Uruguay. Similar variations occur in rates of literacy. In twelve countries less than 20 percent of the adult population were literate in 1975, while sixteen countries had adult literacy rates of 80 percent and over. The quality and extent of basic services also vary widely. In the five best-served countries, there is one nurse for every 432 people; in the five worst-served countries, each nurse serves more than 36,000 people (see table 5).

Between 1960 and 1977 all developing countries improved their provision for basic needs, though at an unequal pace. On the average, life expectancy in low-income countries had risen from 40 years in 1960 to 50 years by 1977; in the advanced industrial countries from 69 to 74; and in the centrally planned economies from 58 to 66. This remarkable decline in mortality rates and the lengthening of life expectancy, without an immediate equivalent decline in fertility rates, caused the rapid rise in population in the developing countries. Similarly, literacy rates were improved. In low-income countries the adult literacy rate rose from 29 percent in 1960 to 36 percent in 1977, in middle-income countries from 51 to 69 percent over the same period.

When trying to relate these improvements statistically to other factors, two relations stand out as significant: past performance and income per head. Countries that did well in 1960 also tended to do well in 1977. Of the sixteen developing countries where life expectancy was more than 60 years in 1960, in fourteen it was more than 70 years in 1977. In no country where life expectancy

2. This section draws on Frances Stewart, "Country Experience in Providing for Basic Needs," *Finance & Development*, vol. 16, no. 4 (December 1979), pp. 23-26.

Table 5. *Provision for Basic Needs in Developing Countries*

Item	Enrollment in primary education as percentage of age group, 1976		Health services, 1976		Percentage of population with access to safe water, 1975	Nutrition, 1974	
	Male	Female	Population per doctor	Population per nurse		Average calories per day	As percentage of requirements[a]
Average of lowest five countries	24	9	56,710	36,764	7	1,773	76
Average of highest five countries[b]	135	127	846	432	89	3,137	125

a. Requirements are defined by the U.N. Food and Agriculture Organization.
b. Among all developing countries, excluding Greece, Israel, Portugal, and Spain.
Source: Data from World Bank, *World Development Report, 1979* (New York: Oxford University Press, 1979); table from Frances Stewart, "Country Experience in Providing for Basic Needs," *Finance & Development,* vol. 16, no. 4 (December 1979).

was less than 60 in 1960 was it more than 70 in 1977. In spite of substantial variations in the rate of improvement among countries over that period, the strong correlation between past and subsequent performance over seventeen years indicates not only the importance of history but also the limits to the scope for large improvements over ten to twenty years.

With some notable exceptions, the second factor related to improved performance is income per head. For a group of eighty-six developing countries in 1975, 52 percent of the variance in life expectancy is related to differences in income per head. Such a relation is, of course, not surprising, for one would expect societies with more resources to devote more of them to the goods and services that prolong life and raise literacy. There is mutual and reinforcing causation between the fulfillment of basic needs and economic performance.

More interesting for the purposes of the basic needs approach is that some countries do much better, and others much worse, than one would predict on the basis of income figures alone. The relation between changes in indicators of basic needs fulfillment is much weaker than that between levels of these indicators to national income. In fact, it was precisely the failure of growth of GNP to eliminate deprivation in that period that led to the new emphasis on basic needs.

One reason for the discrepancies between average income per head and basic needs indicators is that the average conceals what happens to the poorest. For any given average level or growth rate of income, greater equality in the distribution shows better performance in meeting basic needs. The socialist countries, which have more egalitarian income distributions, such as China, Cuba, and North Korea, and the more egalitarian market economies, such as Jamaica, South Korea, Sri Lanka, and Taiwan, do better on basic needs than would be predicted from the income data. The oil exporters and other inegalitarian countries, however, do worse. No country with a very unequal income distribution has done outstandingly well on basic needs. But some countries with highly unequal income distributions are about average in meeting basic needs. Clearly many other factors must also be considered.

The Success Stories

Life expectancy is a useful approximate single indicator of fulfillment of basic needs. One way of identifying the success stories is to draw a line between average income per head and life expectancy for a large number of economies and to note which ones show a higher life expectancy than would be predicted from this average relation. The result is a rather mixed bag: Burma, China, Costa Rica, Cuba, Hong Kong, Jamaica, North Korea, South Korea, Panama, Paraguay, Sri Lanka, Taiwan, Thailand, Uruguay, and Yugoslavia. They vary in size, income per head, growth rates, income distribution, geography, natural resources, history, and political regimes. To get some order into this collection, three institutional and political types may be distinguished: the socialist planned economies such as Cuba, China, and Yugoslavia; some market-oriented economies such as Taiwan and South Korea with special initial conditions of land distribution and special industrialization and trade policies; and the mixed, welfare-oriented economies, of which Sri Lanka is the outstanding success story. Each type followed a different development strategy, yet was successful in meeting basic needs. This suggests that there is no single basic needs strategy, but lessons can be learned from different approaches.

The main component in Cuba's success (life expectancy of 72 years and almost universal literacy) is a high level of public expenditure on education and possibly also health, the benefits of which are widely spread. Cuba spends about twice as much of its national income on health and education as other countries at a similar income level. In addition, basic needs are met by full employment, subsidies for and rationing of essential items such as food, and supply management. The food ration guarantees a well-balanced diet to everybody, and shelter is provided by housing subsidies. In this way, a basic needs package of free education and health services, rationed and subsidized food and institutional feeding, and housing subsidies guarantee the satisfaction of basic needs to all. Participation in the process is achieved through massive political organization. With the possible exception of China, in most socialist, centrally planned economies the satisfaction of basic needs was bought at the expense of some economic growth (and some political rights). Cuban growth over the past fifteen years has been slow.

In China adequate food, shelter, health care, and other basic necessities were provided for the entire population, including the poorest, within a short time with rapid economic growth. Annual growth rates between 1952 and 1978 of 6.2 percent in the aggregate and of 4 percent for income per head exceed substantially the average performance of developing countries. The most important aspect of this achievement is a radical transformation of the institutions on which production is based.

Figures for life expectancy are not available, but crude mortality rates of 27 per thousand population in the 1930s had fallen to 18 per thousand in 1952 and 11 per thousand in 1956. The best-known aspect of China's basic needs effort is its health delivery system. In Ding Xian in Hobei Province a system of village auxiliaries and paramedics supported by trained doctors had brought effective medical care to remote villages at very low cost long before 1949, and these efforts had some impact on the post-1949 policies. But this and similar experiments remained isolated examples.[3]

After the revolution, the emphasis was first on full political mobilization for preventive medicine and the campaign against the four pests: flies, mosquitoes, rats, and sparrows. Later came strikingly successful campaigns for the elimination of schistosomiasis and for family planning. In the mid- and late 1950s emphasis shifted to curative activities. The best-known innovation is the 1.6 million barefoot doctors, rural paramedics with three months to one year of formal training who were chosen from, lived with, and worked in the production brigades. But China is now turning away from the barefoot doctors.

The successful market-oriented economies are exemplified by Taiwan and South Korea. They combine a relatively equal dis-

3. Dwight Perkins, "Rural Health in China" (Washington, D.C.: World Bank, 1979; processed).

tribution of land and income with rapid economic growth. Their primary agent in meeting basic needs has been the growth of personal incomes that permitted expenditure on basic needs goods. The public sector played a supporting role in providing virtually universal primary education and health services, but public expenditure has not been conspicuously large. Whereas in the socialist economies planned production was the driving force in meeting basic needs, in the market-oriented economies it was income generation.

In the third category, the mixed, welfare-oriented economies, Sri Lanka is the outstanding example. Its remarkable performance was initiated in the colonial era, and Sri Lanka has made substantial and rapid improvement in many social indicators since World War II at levels of income per head below $200. Life expectancy is 69 years, and 75 percent of the population are literate. A major factor has been the large public expenditure on primary education, health, and food subsidies. These services have, until recently, been available to the whole population. The food ration accounted for about 20 percent of caloric intake among families with very low incomes. In 1973 the subsidies amounted to about 14 percent of the income of these families. A cutback in food rations in 1974 and a sharp rise in food prices was accompanied by a sharp rise in the death rate. Since the literacy rate, the access to health services, and the quality of water supply had not changed in that year, the importance of the food ration for health is evident. Social programs and food subsidies account for about half of current government expenditure and 10 percent of GDP. Expenditure per head amounts to about $15 a year, but total public expenditure is not remarkably large because of the very small expenditure on defense.

It it commonly believed that Sri Lanka's economy is not viable in the long run because the large public expenditure cannot be sustained and because it reduces economic growth. The programs were in fact sustained, however, with a respectable growth rate, for more than twenty years after World War II. Poor economic management, adverse movement in the terms of trade, and poor monsoons led to severe problems in the 1970s. But with economic reforms and more selective programs for the lower income groups, it appears that Sri Lanka is again able to combine a successful performance in meeting basic needs with economic, growth. The Sri Lankan case shows the importance, for a mixed economy, of consistent and reinforcing efforts on the side of supply (through public sector and production planning), on the side of demand (income generation and transfers), and on the part of institutions (especially public services) for success in meeting basic needs.

Less Successful Countries

The successful routes illustrated above can be complemented by the experiences of less successful countries, which demonstrate what to avoid if basic needs are to be met.

Some of the greatest deficiencies are found among the very poor African countries such as Mali, the Gambia, and Somalia. Income per head there is around $100, literacy rates are low, between 10 and 23 percent; life expectancy is around 40 years; infant mortality is about 200 per thousand. In some areas 50 percent of the children die before they are five years old. More than 75 percent of the population live in rural areas, where malnutrition is chronic, health facilities are poor, and there is little education or safe water. Attempts to move ahead in one sector fail because of the absence of supporting action in others. Providing safe water has little effect without education in hygiene; dirty hands and dirty dishes undo the beneficial results of safe water. Curative health services are ineffective because the environmental causes of ill health—malnutrition and the lack of education and sanitation—set back the cured patient. A concerted attack on several fronts would be more likely to yield results, but these countries lack the resources for such programs and the administrative capacity for a coordinated approach. Outside assistance is therefore essential for success in meeting basic needs.

Consider Somalia. Since 1969 the government of Somalia has been determined to implement an education program. The literacy rate has risen substantially, and many schools have been built, often with the cooperation of rural people. Yet the primary school enrollment ratio remains only 45 percent, and the government is running into severe financial problems owing to the high recurrent costs.

In the Gambia income per head is low (less than $200 in 1977), life expectancy is 33 years, malnutrition is widespread, affecting mainly children and pregnant and nursing women, half the children die before they are five, and the infant mortality rate is more than 200 per thousand live births. There is a high incidence of water-borne and water-related diseases, the literacy rate is 10 percent, primary school enrollment in rural areas is 20 percent, and medical personnel are few and inadequately trained. Yet the country is a substantial net exporter of food. Were it not for these exports, the Gambia would be more than self-sufficient in food production.

These very poor countries have to rely on foreign aid to increase domestic production. The household plays an important part in food production and in determining nutritional and health practices. Efforts to improve the productivity of households are particularly important as part of a basic needs approach.

At the other end of the scale are countries that have registered high rates of economic growth for long periods without much impact on meeting basic needs. Brazil and Indonesia are illustrations. Although Brazil had an average income per head of $1,300 and Indonesia $280 in 1976, both countries have enjoyed high growth rates in recent years, and both have disappointing records in meeting basic needs. The cause must be sought in the pattern and distribution of economic growth and in the design and incidence of public services. Inequality in a setting of high growth need not conflict with meeting basic needs. As long as the absolute level of living of the poor rises, a more rapid rise in the incomes of the better-off need not stand in the way and may even help. But, though the data are not conclusive, the absolute incomes of the very poor may have actually declined. In any case, basic needs have not been met at the rate that one would have expected from the rapid aggregate growth rates.

Because the pattern of growth was largely capital-intensive, employment lagged behind the growth in production and productivity. Continuing high rates of population growth increased the supply of labor, which outpaced demand. Much of the production was directed toward luxury goods, not necessities. The pattern of income generation led to inadequate purchasing power by the poor, and the pattern of production was not adjusted to basic needs. Food prices in particular tended to rise more than the average price level, and even the consumption pattern of the poor deviated from goods and services appropriate to meet basic needs.

Public sector expenditure, which might have corrected some of the failures to meet basic needs, instead reinforced the uneven effects of the private sector. Total public expenditure in both countries was low as a proportion of GDP and tended to be concentrated on the middle class as a result of urban and regional biases. In Indonesia, for example, food subsidies were confined to the military and civil services. In Brazil health services tended to be concentrated in large urban hospitals serving middle-class ailments, and the proportion of health expenditure devoted to preventive medicine declined from 87 percent in 1949 to 30 percent in 1975.

Egypt, with about the same income per head of $280 as Indonesia in 1976, provides a similar, though less extreme example. Growth has been more moderate; income inequality has been less acute and does not appear to have increased. But, as in Indonesia and Brazil, the pattern of growth was concentrated on non–basic needs goods. The proportion of public expenditure to national income has been higher in Egypt but also biased in favor of the urban middle class. Food subsidies are twice as high for the urban as for the rural population.

With larger incomes and higher growth rates, Brazil, Indonesia, and Egypt have, in principle, a wider range of options than the poor African countries. Apart from considerations of political feasibility, incentives, and administration, they could have sacrificed non–basic needs consumption for basic needs without making inroads in investment and growth. The political constraints on such policies are illustrated by the role of the public sector in the three countries, which, in contrast to that in Sri Lanka, has paid little attention to basic needs. A high proportion of public expenditure is by itself not sufficient to ensure success in meeting basic needs. Much depends on the design of the public services, on the degree of devolution to local responsibility, and on administrative efficiency. Some have argued that a basic needs approach has most relevance for middle-income countries because a relatively small redeployment of resources can have a large impact on poverty. The obstacles are not physical but political, however, and cast doubt on the possibility of growing first and redistributing later. Concentrated growth has a built-in resistance to meeting basic needs.

6

Lessons from Sector Experience

IT IS COMMON to refer to the core basic needs sectors as those providing food, health services, education, shelter, and water and sanitation.[1] This classification fits the organization of governments into ministries and corresponds to the sector lending programs of agencies and bilateral donors. But the notion of basic needs sectors presents certain analytical difficulties.

First, the identification of specific basic needs sectors is somewhat arbitrary. It raises such difficult issues as who is to determine the basic needs? How should ends (such as health) be separated from means (such as water supply)?

Second, it is possible and in fact quite common to classify certain activities or expenditures under a basic needs sector, although the benefits accrue for non–basic needs to people who are not poor. Third, it is misleading to link certain objectives, such as good health, with corresponding sectors, such as health services. The links between what might broadly be called basic needs sectors and the fulfillment of basic needs are complex and tenuous. The sectors can even be counterproductive to their own objectives, as when illness caused by the medical system or incompetence caused by the educational system makes people less healthy or less capable. Generally, each so-called basic needs sector has an impact, normally positive but sometimes negative, not only directly on the need to which it caters, but also on other basic and non–basic needs. Education not only makes people

1. See Shahid Javed Burki, "Sectoral Priorities for Meeting Basic Needs," *Finance & Development*, vol. 17, no. 1 (March 1980), pp. 18-22.

better educated, it also improves their nutrition and health, their earning power, and the profits of their employers.

In spite of these difficulties, the main elements of a sectoral approach are unquestionable: food and drinking water; the main determinants of health, including health services and sanitation facilities; shelter; and education. World Bank studies have examined specifically five sectors: nutrition, health, education, water and sanitation, and shelter, and this chapter draws on this work. The studies identified the main problems in each sector and formulated the policies needed to meet the basic needs broadly corresponding to each sector.

The first lesson to emerge from the sector studies is that cross-sectional linkages and appropriate substitution and phasing are crucial, both to improve the results and to reduce costs. The second is that human attitudes and motivation, and social institutions, administration, and organization are as important as adequate physical, financial, and fiscal resources and appropriate technology. The structure of government, international organizations, and specialized agencies can obstruct the implementation of a basic needs program inasmuch as their subdivisions—the separate ministries, agencies, and departments—are each responsible for what appears to be a basic needs sector. The professional interests and pressures of doctors, teachers, and sanitation engineers, as much as the political interests of the richer groups, often present barriers to implementation. Third, the technical ease with which a problem can be tackled is often inversely related to its order of importance. For example, it is easy to supplement the diet of schoolchildren through institutional feeding, but nutritionally the most vulnerable group are children below school age. Fourth, the ultimate test of a basic needs program is a country's total commitment to it, and not the proportion of GDP or the budget devoted to basic needs sectors, nor the specific basic needs projects financed by agencies.

Nutrition

The need for food is perhaps the most basic of all needs. The poor must eat, even if they drink unsafe water, are illiterate, and are not inoculated. The poor in the developing countries spend about 70 percent of their total income on food and more than 50 percent of additional income. Lack of adequate food not only makes people hungry and less able to enjoy life, it also reduces their ability and (by causing apathy) their willingness to work. It also makes them more susceptible to disease by reducing their immunity to infection and other environmental stresses. Prolonged malnutrition among babies and children leads to reduced adult stature; severe malnutrition is associated with decreased brain size and cell number, as well as altered brain chemistry. Malnutrition during pregnancy results in low birth weight, which is a particularly important cause of infant mortality. Children who suffer from severe malnutrition show lags in motor activity, hearing, speech, social and personal behavior, problem-solving ability, eye-hand coordination and categorization behavior, even after rehabilitation.

Malnutrition today is not the result of a global shortage of food. Current world production of grain alone could provide everyone with more than 3,000 calories and 65 grams of protein daily. It has been estimated that 2 percent of the world's grain output would be sufficient to eliminate malnutrition among the world's 500 million malnourished.[2] Nor is malnutrition primarily a problem of an imbalance between calories and protein. Most village surveys have found that if energy intake is adequate, protein needs are also satisfied. The problem is one of distribution: among countries, regions, and income groups, between sexes, and within households. In general, it is the very poor, who spend most of their income on food, who suffer most from malnutrition. In many countries more than 40 percent of the population suffer from calorie-deficient diets, and about 15 percent show deficiences of more than 400 calories per day. Within families it appears that children, and in some societies women, particularly when pregnant or lactating, receive inadequate amounts of food. Calorie deficiencies vary by geographical area, season, and year. To the extent to which global income distribu-

2. Shlomo Reutlinger and Marcelo Selowsky, *Malnutrition and Poverty: Magnitude and Policy Options* (Baltimore, Md.: Johns Hopkins University Press, 1976). If the criticism that the authors overestimate malnutrition is valid, the proportion would be even less.

tion cannot be altered, substantially increased production of basic foodstuffs in the developing countries must form the most important part of the solution. (Food availability in the developing countries increased slightly from 208 kilograms per head in 1961 to 218 kilograms in 1976). The other part of the solution is adequate incomes of the poor, including both production for their own consumption and cash to buy food. For farmers this means security of tenure or ownership of land, a regular outlet for sales, and a supply of credit. Extra food production is necessary to meet the additional demand created by population growth and higher incomes per head, and to prevent soaring food prices from canceling the effects of higher purchasing power. But growth of incomes and food production, important though it is, is not sufficient to eliminate malnutrition within the next twenty years.[3]

Receiving more food does not necessarily meet the basic needs of poor people. It may simply meet the needs of the parasites in their stomachs or of the moneylenders. Malnutrition is a problem of the pathology of the environment, and increasing food intake by itself may not help. Cases have been recorded where it has made things worse, because the extra food consumption of the earning members of families was matched by extra physical efforts, and the rest of the family got less.[4] It may be not food that is needed, but education, safe water, medical services, or a land reform to permit people to make better use of the available food supply.

Raising the real incomes of the poor so that they can buy more food is clearly one important way of improving nutrition. But

3. To achieve perfect nutritional standards is virtually impossible, and a reasonable objective is to reduce the significant handicaps from nutritional deficiency. Many people in rich countries present medical problems from being overweight and obese, but no great social significance is attached to these ills. There may be as many as 7 million Americans suffering from malnutrition. In poor countries, people have adapted to mild cases of calorie deficiency by attaining a lower weight and height, by being less active, and, in the case of women, by ovulating less regularly.

4. Daniel R. Gross and Barbara A. Underwood, "Technological Change and Caloric Costs: Sisal Agriculture in Northeastern Brazil," *American Anthropolgist,* vol. 73, no. 3 (June 1971), pp. 725-40.

this is a slow process, and there are speedier and more direct ways. Iodine deficiency, which can cause goiter, apathy, and proneness to other diseases, is easily remedied by iodizing salt. More difficult to remedy are deficiencies in vitamin A, which can cause blindness and death in children, and in iron, which leads to anemia and reduced productivity. Protein-energy malnutrition, which may cause irreversible brain damage in children and apathy in adults, is the most difficult to remedy. Yet, it is the most serious problem in malnutrition, followed by deficiencies in iron and vitamin A.

Apart from the emergency of famine, nutrition policies for the chronically malnourished poor call for a long-term, sustained effort. Intervention can take the form of agricultural policy, supplementary feeding, food fortification programs, food sub-sidies and rationing, and complementary policies in nonfood sectors.

Since the poor and the rich do not spend their money on the same kind of food, policies that encourage greater production of poor people's food—such as cassava, corn, sorghum, and mil-let—can help reduce malnutrition. Food marketing and storage programs can reduce regional, seasonal, and annual variations in supplies and prices. Policies to encourage production of food for the poor should extend to all aspects of agricultural policy, including research, extension programs, credit, and marketing.

Supplementary feeding may take place in schools, at work, or at clinics for pregnant or lactating women. With the receipt of extra institutional food, however, meals at home may be cur-tailed, so that the vulnerable groups do not get much additional food, and, at least in the case of schoolchildren, these programs do not reach the groups particularly at risk, such as children below school age. Here again, the ease of intervention (because schools already exist and delivery is cheap) is inversely related to its importance. Food supplementation at the work place, if neith-er the food nor the extra energy is diverted to other activities, serves both a basic need and productivity.

Special foods and food fortification, as in the case of protein and vitamin fortification and salt iodization, have been successful up to a point, though they meet with both technical and political difficulties. General subsidies to food are very expensive, absorbing up to 20 percent of budgetary expenditure in some countries, and selective ones such as food stamps are difficult to administer. Programs are easier and cheaper to administer if the subsidies are for food that is eaten only by the poor. Rich countries tend to tax poor food consumers to subsidize relatively better-off farmers. Poor countries tend to tax poor farmers to subsidize food such as high-quality wheat and rice that is consumed by the better-off urban groups, though among the poorest are landless laborers and urban dwellers who have to buy food. An efficient and equitable system of subsidies to poor consumers that does not penalize poor producers of food is both administratively and politically difficult. But when agricultural prices are increased as an incentive for production, measures should be taken to prevent greater malnutrition among landless laborers. Some countries have successfully overcome these difficulties.

Enough has been said elsewhere about linkages to show that policies in sectors other than food are essential for better nutrition. Safe water and the prevention of intestinal diseases would enable people to absorb the same amount of food more effectively. Education can help people spend their money more wisely and prepare food more economically and hygienically; they can learn to complement their present diet with local food. The battle against early weaning and the use of baby formulas has hit the headlines, but the desire of women to cease breast feeding is often part of the general process of modernization and the desire to emulate the more advanced groups in the country.

Malnutrition is the result of a complex set of conditions, all stemming from poverty. But although most people suffering from calorie deficiencies are poor, not all poor people suffer from such deficiencies. Some quite high-income countries and groups of people suffer from considerable malnutrition, and some low-income countries have none. This is one of the hopeful messages of the basic needs approach.

Health

It is often said that better health and longer lives accelerate population growth and imply a return to the Malthusian trap. It is, of course, true that the drop in mortality rates, which lengthened life expectancy, has been a major cause of population growth, since fertility did not fall in step.

Recent evidence, however, suggests that high rates of infant mortality are a main reason parents want large families and that they may even overinsure against the risk of their children's death. Anything that reduces infant mortality removes this motive, tends to reduce fertility, and, after a time lag, may lower the rate of population growth.[5] The time lag between reduced infant mortality and reduced fertility is likely to be shortened when the decline in mortality is associated with factors such as women's education and improvements in health that also directly reduce fertility. More generally, improvements in health and education, in addition to directly meeting a basic need, are an effective and relatively low-cost method of weakening the link between poverty and rapid population growth.

The World Health Organization defines health as "a state of complete physical, mental, and social well-being and not merely the absence of disease or infirmity."[6] On this broad definition health can be identified as a basic need. All the rest on the list of basic needs are "inputs" into the process that "produces" health.

Life expectancy and infant mortality are very imperfect indicators of this state of full health. But a drop in mortality, which

5. The evidence for this is uncertain and disputed. For a contrary view, see Nick Eberstadt "Recent Declines in Fertility in Less Developed Countries," *World Development,* vol. 8, no. 1 (January 1980), pp. 37–60, and the sources cited there. The causal nexus may go the other way: high fertility may be accompanied by the acceptance or even the unconscious encouragement of high infant mortality. In that case it would seem that high infant mortality points to readiness for family planning, rather than that reduced mortality makes family planning acceptable. See Susan C. M. Scrimshaw, "Infant Mortality and Behavior in the Regulation of Family Size," *Population and Development Review,* vol. 4, no. 3 (September 1978), pp. 383–403.

6. Constitution of the World Health Organization (Geneva, 1946).

Table 6. *Life Expectancy at Birth*
(years)

Income group *(1977* GNP *per capita)*[a]	*1960*	*1970*	*1977*
Low income (up to $300)	42	47	50
Middle income (more than $300)	53	57	60
All developing countries	47	51	54
Industrialized countries	69	72	74

a. According to the classification of the World Bank, *World Development Report, 1979* (New York: Oxford University Press, 1979). The developing countries exclude those with population below 1 million as well as the capital-surplus oil exporters.

leads to a longer life expectancy, is certainly desired by everyone. And a fall in infant mortality, even if it does not show up in figures of higher incomes, certainly does show up in the eyes and hearts of parents. People in the developing countries are now living longer than they did twenty years ago, largely because of the control of communicable diseases such as cholera and malaria. The complete elimination of smallpox was achieved in the 1970s.

In developing countries as a group, life expectancy is about 53 years, but there are large regional differences. In Africa it is about 47 years, in South Asia 49 years, and in Latin America about 61 years. By contrast, in Western Europe and North America it is about 72 years (see table 6). This gap is largely due to very high death rates among children. In the poorest regions of the poorest countries half of all children die before the age of five. In Africa the infant mortality rate is over 100 deaths per thousand births compared with 15 per thousand in developed countries. In developing countries children between one and five years are twelve to fifteen times more likely to die than children born in developed countries. Among survivors, though their life expectancy is only six to eight years less than in developed countries, disability, debility, and temporary incapacity seriously diminish the enjoyment of life and the ability to work. Blindness afflicts 30 million to 40 million people, and river blindness, vitamin A deficiency, and water-borne infections threaten the sight of many more. It is estimated that a tenth of the lifetime of the average person in a developing country is seriously disrupted by ill health.

The major killers of small children are gastrointestinal and respiratory infections, measles, and malnutrition—conditions for which inexpensive prevention or treatment is technically possible. The principal nonfatal diseases in developing countries are gastrointestinal and respiratory infections, skin diseases, and the main tropical diseases. Accidental injuries are also rapidly becoming major health hazards.

There are substantial differences in health between urban and rural areas within developing countries. The crude death rate for 1960 in the rural areas of the developing countries was estimated by the United Nations at 21.7 per thousand, compared with 15.4 for urban areas. The situation is the opposite of that in nineteenth-century England, when death rates in the cities were higher than in the country. Town people today enjoy comparatively better health because of higher incomes, better sanitation and water supply, greater literacy, and better personal health services.

Health services receive high priority in all developing countries, most of which have publicly financed health care systems and programs of investment in sanitation, water supply, and health education. If private expenditures and certain indirect costs, such as those for transport and training health workers, are included in the total, 6 to 10 percent of GDP is spent on health care. This amounts to about $75 billion annually for the developing countries as a whole. (More narrowly defined, however, public expenditure on health is only 1 to 3 percent of GDP.) Additional sums are spent on family planning, water supply, sanitation, and nutrition.

With a few notable exceptions, health care systems in developing countries have been patterned on those in the advanced industrial countries. The emphasis is on the institutional care of the sick. This bias in favor of curative and against preventive health services is understandable. The cure of actual victims of disease is a visible response to identifiable suffering, whereas no one knows whose lives have been saved and whose suffering has been spared by preventive measures. Cures relieve real suffering and save real lives, prevention relieves only statistical suffering and saves statistical lives. It is not surprising that policymakers often prefer the former to the latter. In recent years, however, there have been signs of a shift of health care to previously underserved populations, particularly in the countryside, and to preventive health services.

Evidence is now accumulating that primary health care can be efficiently provided at costs that can be afforded. According to pilot studies, primary health care for all need not cost more than $2.50 to $4 per person a year. But in spite of large expenditures and the technical possibility of solving many of the most common health problems, efforts to improve health have had only modest success. The main reasons for this are generally well known. They include emphasis on curative at the expense of preventive care and on sophisticated hospital facilities at the expense of primary health services; health facilities that are concentrated in or near towns (in Brazil urban dwellers receive health subsidies five times as large as those of rural people) and are inaccessible to those, especially women and children, in distant rural areas; inappropriate training for doctors and health workers that neglects local health problems; the unreliable supply of drugs, pesticides, and other provisions in remote areas; the inability to pay for treatment at a clinic or to stay away from work; resistance to medical services that are not socially acceptable or not perceived as useful; the absence of integration with other basic needs sectors; and the lack of local participation in setting up and managing a program.

Many of these problems have their roots in the design and implementation of health policies. Programs to train manpower and build health facilities are often devised without sufficient understanding of the long-run implications for recurrent costs, or of the immediate requirements for complementary investment in supervision, transport, equipment, and supplies. Laws and regulations are often incompatible with basic health care. For example, training and licensing requirements for health workers often prohibit the use of medical auxiliaries to run village health facilities or to administer injections. Procedures for the procurement, distribution, and control of supplies and staff allow corruption and waste and do not assure reliability of service.

The solution of these problems lies in a strong commitment to a simple, community-level health care system. To be successful, the commitment must come from both the central government and the local communities, and political pressures must be mobilized to weaken the urban bias and the vested interest of the professionals. Experience demonstrates that village health workers can be trained at low costs and that cheap, preventive, mass rural health services can be implemented.

A successful community health service requires careful decisions as to which problems are to be handled by the village, which by the local clinic, and which by the hospital and how problems are to be referred upward. In addition, the village health workers need good supervision and technical support, including continuing education and training. The service needs to be reliably supported by better forward planning, control and maintenance of vehicles, rigorous management of inventories, and adequate financing. Also important are participation by the community in the design and construction of facilities, cooperative efforts to finance drug purchases, unpaid volunteer workers and contributions of building materials, community selection of health workers from among members of the community, and local participation in decisions affecting health.

As emphasized repeatedly, the successful design and implementation of a health care system also depends crucially on action in other basic needs sectors. The effectiveness of the health sector depends on education of the poor in basic hygiene and health, education and training of doctors and health workers, and improved management and research capacity; it depends on nutrition, water and sanitation, and shelter. Such integration has to take place at the national, district, and local level—and there are opportunities for international involvement as well, as will be argued in chapter 8.

Education

Education plays many roles in the development process. It is itself a basic need because it enhances the people's understanding of themselves, their society, and their natural environment and gives them access to their cultural heritage. It improves living skills, increases productivity by improving work skills, and lowers reproductivity by raising women's status. Perhaps the greatest value of education at low levels of living lies in its contribution to meeting other basic needs. Education can greatly reduce the cost of nutrition, health, and water and sanitation programs. Although precise costs depend on circumstances, savings by a factor of ten to twenty are likely if behavioral changes resulting from education can be built into other programs.

Education also meets non–basic needs of both the educated and their employers. The division of the gains will depend on whether macroeconomic policies and structural changes ensure that the nonpoor do not capture the improvements in human capital. Education can be hostile to the satisfaction of basic needs when it creates aspirations in excess of those that can be met and contributes to educated unemployment, brain drain, or the loss of common sense and the creation of anti–basic needs political constituencies that sometimes go with professionalization.

Education makes people more adaptable by giving them a base of knowledge, skills, attitudes, and valuations—a wider field of information on which to draw. It plays an enormously important part in determining the nature and quality of an individual's life and work. Education is a process and the end product is an achievement. The process of education contains an element of a consumption good, insofar as it is enjoyed for its own sake, but it is also analogous to a productive process, the result of which is a durable good. The achievement partakes in the nature of a durable producer good; it is like a machine. As such, education can raise the income of individuals and the production of society above what it would otherwise have been. And it is also like a durable consumer good because it enables the educated person to enjoy books, works of art, nature, and other people more fully.

In its aspect of a durable producer good it not only contributes to marketed services but it also raises the productivity of people in their homes and in all nonmarket production. Ability to read makes people able to build better cooking stoves, or thatch their huts better, or heat water with less fuel, or prepare more nutritious meals, or improve their sanitary practices. In designing and implementing a basic needs program for the education sector, all these roles have to be taken into account.

There has been substantial progress in organized education in the developing countries since 1960. The number of students enrolled increased from 142 million in 1960 to 315 million in 1975. Primary enrollment doubled, secondary enrollment tripled, and tertiary enrollment quadrupled. In those fifteen years about 400 million people have become literate.

This apparently dramatic progress hides some disquieting features. First, the figures are not very reliable and tend to exaggerate functional literacy and enrollment. Second, the rate of expansion has declined steadily between 1960 and 1975 in all developing countries, with the sharpest decline at the primary level. Third, there are now about 850 million people (250 million children and 600 million adults, of whom 400 million are women) in the developing countries who have had little or no access to formal schooling. For each of the 315 million now enrolled in schools, there are about three without education. Most of these are among the 770 million poorest people in the world. Illiteracy is concentrated in the poorest countries. Of the thirty-four countries in which adult illiteracy rates are over 70 percent, twenty-two belong to the lowest-income group (see table 7).

Expansion of basic educational opportunities for both children and adults is perhaps the most important task for educational planners in the Third World. Other urgent issues include inequalities in enrollment opportunities, the need to improve the quality and usefulness of the education and the effectiveness of the system, and the problem of cost.

Many educational systems discriminate against women, rural residents, communities distant from the capital, adults, the poor, and sometimes people from certain ethnic origins. From the

Table 7. *Adult Literacy Rates*
(percent)

Income group (1977 GNP per capita)[a]	1960	1970	1975
Low income (up to $300)	28	35	39
Middle income (more than $300)	56	65	71
All developing countries	39	46	51
Industrialized countries	98	99	99

a. According to the classification of the World Bank, *World Development Report, 1979* (New York: Oxford University Press, 1979). The developing countries exclude those with population below 1 million as well as the capital-surplus oil exporters.

point of view of meeting basic needs, the most significant disparity is the unequal access for girls and women. These disparities are far greater in developing than in industrial countries. In 1975 in developing countries the primary school enrollment ratio for boys was 70 percent, that for girls only 53 percent. For secondary schools the ratio was 42 percent for boys and 28 percent for girls. For ages 18 to 23, 11 percent for boys and 6 percent for girls. These averages conceal extremely low female enrollment ratios for some countries. For example, female enrollment for the 6–11 age group in 1975 was 4.7 percent in the Yemen Arab Republic, 4.8 percent in Afghanistan, and 10.3 percent in Nepal. The corresponding male enrollment ratios in these countries were 33.4, 25.8, and 43.5 percent respectively.

It is very difficult to compare the quality of education. International comparative studies that investigate educational curriculums, teaching qualifications and methods, educational materials, and years of schooling seem to show, however, that the quality of education is much lower in most developing countries than in industrial ones. In most developing countries there are also large variations in the quality of education received by different groups, and large discrepancies between what is taught at school and what is needed for life and work. The numbers of students attending school is below what the resources and facilities would permit in many countries. On average, only half of primary school entrants reach the fourth grade, and about 15 to 20 percent of school places are occupied by repeaters. Irregular attendance, repeating, and dropping out represent a huge waste of resources. Most developing countries lack the capabilities to plan, manage, and do the research required for the successful formulation, implementation, and evaluation of policy.

The expansion and equalization of educational opportunities call for the more efficient use of existing facilities and the creation of new capacity. To increase the efficient use of existing facilities it is necessary to reduce the wastage of repetitions and dropouts and to make fuller use of buildings and equipment by multiple shifts and summer sessions. Financial assistance could make opportunities more equal; the services of other than fully qualified teachers (public servants, students, workers, retired people) could be used to expand capacity; and resources could be shifted from higher to lower levels of education, subject to adequate provision for training teachers and other professional manpower.

To create new capacity local initiatives should be encouraged and supported. Adult education and family education programs, particularly those related to basic needs, should be expanded. Adult education would shorten the period before literacy becomes universal and would make the schooling of children more effective. In some regions it has been found that children's school attendance is related not so much to content or the incomes of parents as to the level of education of the mothers. Mass media and distance-teaching techniques should be adopted; and preschool child development programs should be expanded, with highest priority to the children of the poor.

The quality of educational services can be improved by making curriculums and teacher training programs more relevant to the basic needs of the poor. There is a need to raise living and working skills, to make learning more responsive to the needs of society, and to increase the adaptability and flexibility of the people. The educational system in general can be made more efficient by better planning and management and by improving the home and other out-of-school environments of children, an improvement to which adult education can contribute.

The size of the educational task is daunting and its costs are formidable. Although poor countries typically have perhaps one-tenth the national income of rich countries, the proportion of the population aged 5 to 15 and to be educated is perhaps twice as large as in rich countries (25 to 30 percent compared with about 15 percent). Teachers' salaries, which are near or below the national average income in rich countries, are four or five times (in Africa seven times) the average in poor countries. This means that a vastly greater share (typically eight to ten times as much) of a much smaller national cake and government budget would have to be devoted to education, with the inevitable result that less would be left over to implement other objectives.

Quite apart from the constraint set by available resources, the social and economic results of such a program need to be considered. In Africa and Asia the experience has been that a very high proportion, sometimes as much as four-fifths, of those educated in primary schools drop out or forget what they learn soon after, so that educational efforts and expenditure on them are wasted. Those who remember what they are taught seek to escape their miserable rural existence and hope to find employment as clerks in the towns. There are not enough administrative jobs for all of them, and, far from becoming a source of productive activity, the educated unemployed are liable to become a source of disruptive activity. The problem concerns almost every developing country: primary school leavers in Africa, high school leavers in West Asia, and university graduates in South Asia.

In view of this large demand on financial resources, governments may either try to raise additional resources or reduce costs by raising efficiency. There are four possible sources of funds. First, education may be partly self-financed, as in the case of the Cuban agricultural schools, which contribute to the school budget, to national production, and to exports; or some of the costs of education can be shared by employers. Second, local communities may mobilize their underutilized resources, such as land, labor, and building materials, and may also contribute to the recurrent costs of the schools. Third, fees may be charged and loans extended to postelementary students, with scholarships for the poor. In communities where people do not earn wages, fees could be collected in kind. Fourth, foreign aid can contribute to capital and recurrent costs, especially teachers' salaries.

Cost reductions that do not reduce the quality of education are not easy. Improvements that reduce the number of dropouts and of repeaters would reduce unit costs. Reallocation within the system from higher to lower levels (in Egypt, for example, 30 percent of the education budget goes to university education) and from building to staff may sometimes be possible. Cost saving at the higher level is also possible by better use of staff and space, accelerated courses, greater selectivity of students, and improved management. Even a small percentage saved in secondary and tertiary education would yield substantial funds for expanding basic education, although the training of teachers and other needed professionals must not be neglected.

Water and Sanitation

Adequate supplies of safe water and a sanitary system of waste disposal are important elements in human health. According to the World Health Organization, diseases related to unsafe water supply and poor sanitation rank among the top three causes of morbidity and mortality in most developing countries.

One to two liters of water daily is a physiological necessity; without it, people cannot survive. For a reasonable minimum standard of living, people need twenty-five to forty liters daily of convenient and safe water for drinking, food preparation, and personal hygiene. The easy availability of water spares women the time-consuming task of fetching it and frees them for more productive work and for more attention to meeting basic needs.

The disposal of human waste in such a way as to remove it from human contact is also important for health. In many rural areas this can be accomplished without much investment. In most urban areas, however, where population is more concentrated, a higher level of waste disposal facilities is often required to protect community health and prevent environmental degradation. Costs vary widely, depending on the techniques of transport, treatment, and disposal or re-use of waste.

The supply of water and sewerage services has expanded in some areas during the past twenty-five years, but the quality of service in many places has declined dramatically. World Bank estimates suggest that fewer than 500 million of the 2,500 million people in the developing countries have access to adequate supplies of safe water; the number without access is growing by 70 million every year. The percentage (25 to 27 percent) of people served with waste disposal facilities has not increased substantially. Recent estimates put the capital cost of achieving universal access to adequate water supplies and sanitation facilities between $200 billion and $600 billion. To achieve this by 1990—the target adopted by the 1977 World Water Conference—would mean that annual investment for water would have to double for urban areas and quadruple for rural areas, while annual investment for waste disposal must double and increase eightfold for urban and rural areas, respectively.

To meet basic needs in water and sanitation facilities, many issues must be resolved. These may be roughly divided into the "hardware" questions of appropriate water delivery and waste disposal systems and standards of water quality, and the "software" questions of institution building, training and health education, and financing.

Water Supply Systems

The main issue is the type of delivery system to be installed. In urban areas the alternatives are house connections or some combination of house connections and standpipes. Many developing countries want to copy the systems now used in the industrialized nations; that is, a centrally controlled and treated source of water, wide-ranging transmission lines, and metered, multiple-tap connections in every house or apartment. But such advanced systems are not recommended for developing countries because of the high cost. Public standpipes are a more appropriate technology in areas where water has to be distributed to a large number of people at minimum cost. For rural communities the main alternatives are communal systems with standpipes or properly located and constructed village wells and springs. Simple standpipes or wells cost about $10 per person in rural areas; the costs for house connections rise to $75 in rural areas and twice that in urban areas.

Water Quality

It is often argued that the cost of meeting drinking water standards, such as those recommended by the World Health Organization, is prohibitive. In many rural areas, however, groundwater is safe for drinking without treatment, or surface water can be processed by a low-cost infiltration system. Where these options are not feasible, it is necessary to construct facilities for sedimentation, filtration, and disinfection.

Waste Disposal Systems

A properly located, constructed, and maintained latrine will meet all public health requirements for the sanitary disposal of human waste whatever the design, be it a simple vault or borehole, one with a complex water seal, a multiple vault unit, or a conventional water flush system. Costs vary between about $5 per person in rural areas and $15 to $200 in towns, depending on whether sewerage is included.[7] No one design is better for health than another; the preference depends on a composite of cultural, aesthetic, social, technical, and cost factors.

One major conclusion of research is that there are "sanitation sequences": step-by-step improvements that lead from one option to another and are designed to minimize costs over the whole sequence. A community can select initially one of the low-cost technologies (for example, a pit latrine) in the knowledge that, with economic progress, the technology can be upgraded to a pour-flush lavatory with soakaway, then to one with a small base sewer, and eventually to a modified system of conventional sewerage. This is not possible if conventional water-borne sewerage is adopted. From the outset it calls for large

---

7. In the Philippines rudimentary rural privies were built at a cost of less than $1 each, excluding self-help labor. This was equivalent to a cost of about 15 cents per person.

investment and large flows, which dispose largely of sullage and are not an economic solution.

Since a wide range of options for sewerage does exist, why have appropriate technologies not been more widely adopted? The answer is partly lack of information, but largely that professionals are not trained or motivated to adopt unconventional solutions. Another reason is the absence of administrative structures that involve the local communities in selecting, building, and maintaining the facilities they use. Furthermore, financial costs make sewerage appear cheaper than its true economic costs, because capital is often undervalued and labor overvalued.

Institution Building, Training, and Education

World Bank experience suggests that most developing countries do not now have the capacity to design, prepare, and construct an increasing number of water supply and waste disposal facilities or properly manage, operate, and maintain them. The lack of trained people and of institutional competence is a far more serious obstacle than the lack of finance. There is an urgent need for training and institution building.

Health education is also critically important. One individual in a community can contaminate an otherwise safe system. The critical issue in water and sanitation may be not so much financial resources or administrative and engineering capacity as fairly simple behavioral changes, so that existing and future facilities have a much more immediate and effective impact on health. Because water for cleaning does not have to meet the same standards as water for drinking and cooking, teaching people to boil a small amount of water for drinking could mean a substantial saving in cost. But it is not easy to teach people to keep the drinking water in separate containers, and thirsty children tend to drink whatever water is available. Moreover, the substitution of education for a safe water supply is not cheap: kerosene to boil the water would cost at least $20 a year.

In rural areas, to secure the necessary financial, administrative, and maintenance commitment, it is particularly important that those benefiting from a water supply or waste disposal project participate in decisions on the type of supply, the methods of construction, operation, and maintenance, and the system of tariffs and charges.

Financing

The appropriate pricing system for water supply and waste disposal is difficult to determine. To secure economic efficiency, it is desirable to relate tariffs to marginal costs. Such a pricing system may involve heavy administrative costs, however. And where marginal costs are low in relation to total costs, the system has to be supplemented by charging for overhead costs to avoid a financial deficit. There are also considerations of equity, ability to pay, and access. A system of pricing based on cost recovery might debar very poor consumers from using the service and would thus be at odds with the philosophy of universal access. It is then necessary to consider schemes of cross-subsidization from rich to poor consumers and from rich to poor areas. Such schemes might conflict with principles of marginal cost pricing.

Shelter

In both urban and rural areas there is a need for shelter of a reasonable standard to protect health and provide a tolerable environment in which people can live. But the basic need for urban shelter is more acute. Rapid urbanization is expected to continue over the next few decades, doubling the number of very poor households between 1980 and 2000, while the number of poor households in rural areas may decline. Moreover, the supply of land and building materials is much more deficient in urban areas, and the health hazards presented by poor accommodations are greater. The chief emphasis of a basic needs program is thus on urban housing, although the need for upgrading accommodations in rural areas should not be neglected.

Meeting basic needs for shelter is well within the resource constraints of most developing countries. The shelter sector is not, as is sometimes said, a bottomless pit into which scarce resources must be poured unendingly. On average, a 0.8 percent increase in the share of GNP devoted to housing worldwide (now between 3 and 6 percent in most countries) would suffice to provide adequate urban shelter for low-income groups by the year 2000.

The basic need for shelter of all but the bottom tenth to fifth of the income distribution (clearly an important qualification) can be met through programs that emphasize homeownership. Shelter needs of the poorest 10 to 20 percent, however, can be met only by making more rental accommodations available and by subsidy programs. Except for the poorest, income is seldom the binding constraint, and the major problems in providing shelter therefore do not lie on the side of effective demand. The consumption of adequate shelter is low because its price is high owing to shortcomings in the supply of land, public services, and financing.

There is not a shortage of land as such, but rather there is difficulty in making the land available for the construction of shelters, especially for low-income groups. The problem is almost exclusively urban and mostly institutional: typically, a few landlords have monopoly powers, and there are confused titles, cumbersome legal systems, and unrealistic costs involved in land transfers. Without security of tenure, the poor will not make the necessary investments to improve their housing.

The delivery of public services is particularly important to low-income housing because water supply, electricity, sewerage, transport, and education account for a high proportion of the cost of shelter. Most governments have not extended services rapidly enough to meet the needs of the low-income settlements that surround most urban areas. Furthermore, although low subsidized tariffs for government services are often justified as benefiting the poor, they have frequently misfired because of supply limitations. It is common to find, for example, the poor buying water from vendors and paying from ten to twenty times the subsidized amount paid by higher-income groups, who are connected to the public water supply system.

In most countries, little financing is available for low-income housing. Some finance, usually highly subsidized, is lent through public sector institutions and is available only for public-sponsored housing. The bulk of low-income housing is financed out of the savings of the households themselves, without any financial intermediary. One important reason for the absence of mortgage lending is the insecurity of tenure of the borrower.

Most of the problems of the shelter sector are thus the institutional barriers to the acquisition of land and access to mortgage finance. In addition to removing these barriers, the public sector should concentrate on improving the supply of public services— not of housing as such. Generally, the poor are able to construct their own dwellings, but they cannot provide the services to go with them. In supplying services, cost recovery is generally desirable to keep standards down to affordable levels, ensure replicability, and prevent the accumulation of enormous financial burdens. If cities are to improve their capacity to absorb the inevitable large increases in population, efficient management is essential and should deal more with the packaging of services than the delivery of any one service. The packaging of services— that is, the combined provision of water, sanitation, and transport—particularly when linked to land tenure, broadens the scope for cross-subsidies and income transfers within the community and improves the prospects for cost recovery.

7

What Have We Learned?

THE SECTORAL STUDIES of the World Bank fall into two categories: those primarily concerned with the public sector production and delivery of services such as education, health, and water, and those concerned with sectoral interventions that supplement or influence private decisions, as in the case of nutrition and shelter. The distinction is not hard and fast, for usually the goods and services supplied by the public sector (such as education, medical services, and drinking water) are also available in the private market, and there are public elements in the sectors in which market decisions dominate. The work on public sector production has stressed adequate supply, of the right kind, to the people in need. Demand also plays an important role (for example, parents must be willing and able to send their children, especially girls, to school), but the emphasis is on supply. By contrast, the experience with nutrition and shelter underscores the need for adequate effective demand.

There are, however, important differences in the conclusions of the work on nutrition and on shelter, the two private basic needs sectors. Waiting for incomes to rise until hunger and malnutrition are eradicated would take too long, and it is concluded that interventions such as subsidies can shorten the process. In the case of shelter, however, except for the poorest 10 to 20 percent, the conclusion is that acceptable solutions can be found within the income constraint even in the poorest countries. The difference, of course, stems largely from the different definitions of basic needs. Basic needs for food are determined by quasi-scientific caloric requirements; for shelter, by contrast, if they are determined partly by "affordability" the conclusion becomes almost a tautology—"almost," because the demand for shelter is much more compressible than the need for food. Much of the work on shelter draws on more conventional economic arguments for reducing imperfections in the working of markets in order to reach the poor. It is not subsidies but the "restraint of restraints" that will enable the poor to buy adequate shelter. In contrast, the nutrition work starts from an objective standard of food consumption and concludes that direct interventions (such as subsidies or institutional feeding) are necessary to meet needs. Of course, increased food production and higher incomes also play an important part, but the central concern is with how to reconcile subsidizing food to consumers with giving adequate incentives to food producers.

In addition to the distinction between public supply and private market choices there is another differentiation between two approaches. One is to reinforce the existing desires and behavior of consumers and citizens (whether these desires are expressed in market choices or at the ballot box), and the other is to change the behavior of individuals through interventions. In shelter the thrust is for the former, in nutrition and in water and sanitation for the latter. Both the technocratic determination of basic nutritional needs as so many calories per head and the affordability approach to shelter imply value judgments. These are likely to differ from the value judgments derived from letting the people choose or from determining social choices some other way.

The difference between the approaches to nutrition and to shelter is the result of not only different ways of determining basic needs but also differences in the scope for government intervention in the two sectors. Since the scope for government intervention varies from country to country, abstract sector work has to be supplemented by country experience. It may be regarded as a fortunate coincidence that in housing, precisely the area in which government is not very efficient, basic needs can be met out of private incomes.

In education, health, and water and sanitation the issue is not intervention in the private sector but public production and delivery. As a result, the principal concern is with the design of the public service and the reallocation of resources from non–

basic to basic needs services. In some cases, the total level of expenditure needs to be increased by diverting resources from the private to the public sector. The two sets of policies raise different administrative and political issues.

Administration and Management of Basic Needs Policy

Institutional, organizational, and administrative problems are encountered in countries that have failed to meet basic needs at all stages of the policy process. The formulation of policy is heavily affected by political considerations, with insufficient understanding of the relations among the administrative and bureaucratic structure, the economy, and the society. It is also often distorted by the excessive standards imposed by the professionals, whether engineers, doctors, or teachers. Policy implementation suffers from inefficient bureaucratic procedures, lack of qualified managerial staff, lack of coordination among national units and between national and local units, and poorly motivated civil servants. Policy evaluation is virtually nonexistent because of inadequate information and the lack of research and experimentation. Basic needs programs impose special administrative requirements (though not of a high order) because they are often somewhat experimental, extending to new areas and involving different procedures.

There is no panacea for the host of institutional problems faced by the developing countries. Most of these issues cannot be disentangled from their social, political, and economic context. In addition to management training, two changes might make basic needs programs more efficient. One is to restructure organizations to fit the functional requirements of the programs. In many cases, this is likely to involve decentralization, but with appropriate links with higher levels and national authorities (as in the organization of health services, for example). New administrative procedures that increase staff participation in decision-making would increase not only staff commitment but also the responsiveness of the program to local needs.

The second change is to increase participation by the poor, for whom the projects are organized, in decisionmaking and the delivery of services. The major beneficiaries are often willing to supply labor, materials, and finance to establish the services. Furthermore, a high degree of participation is far more important in most basic needs programs than in more conventional types of economic activity. In education or health programs, for example, the cooperation of the public or patient is essential; in sanitation programs the choice of technology is closely linked to the degree of local responsibility. In many cases, the participation of women is especially important and may conflict with traditional, generally male-oriented organizational forms. Experimenting with organizational structures and decisionmaking is an important element in developing an effective basic needs approach.

Finance

The question of finance is peculiarly difficult. For many basic needs projects recurrent costs are quite heavy in relation to capital costs. This means that any system must allow for continuing financial support, rather than a once-for-all commitment to capital costs. The obvious solution—levying charges to cover recurrent costs—may be both difficult to administer and undesirable because the social benefits of the projects very often far exceed the private benefits to the individual consumer. This is clearly true, for example, of vaccination programs, health education, or sanitation projects, where the community at large benefits as well as the participating individuals. In other cases it may be difficult to charge for the services because they are provided communally and the benefits are not easily assigned. Since a major objective of basic needs programs is to provide universal access—especially for the very poor—any system of charges is likely to debar the very people for whom the programs are essential. Despite these problems, unless some system of generating finance on a continual basis is intrinsic to the programs, they are liable to be limited in coverage and in duration, as the central government becomes overburdened with the fiscal load.

Experience with the financial problems of the individual sectors suggests that in some areas charges to cover recurrent costs are reasonable and compatible with social and economic efficiency. In the case of shelter, water, sanitation, and some recurrent medical costs, charges probably offer the best solution, but they should not be levied—or should be levied at much reduced rates—on the poorest consumers. The poor may be financed by cross-subsidization from richer consumers or from general government revenues. In programs for which user charges are not desirable or feasible as a system of finance—as for much of education and health—planning for the finance of recurrent costs should be intrinsic to the projects. If, as often happens, the local community takes on responsibility for some portion of the capital costs, it may also be able and prepared to make a similar commitment for recurrent costs. The same goes for aid donors. It should not be assumed that the central government will automatically pay 100 percent of the recurrent costs of this type of project.

Central government financing is likely to be required for subsidies in the case of nutrition programs and other services for poor consumers. To limit the government's financial responsibility requires careful targeting to confine the subsidies to those most in need. Effective targeting is very difficult for administrative and political reasons and may be easier for some programs—such as subsidies on food consumed primarily by the very poor—than for others. Larger subsidies on an appropriate product might be used in preference to small subsidies on several products, each requiring complex administrative procedures.

Difficult though it is in many countries to raise the real resources and the fiscal resources for the social sectors, expenditure is not the main constraint. Egypt's education budget is now about 10 percent of GDP, yet average literacy rates are only 44 percent and primary school enrollment 76 percent. Mali is spending about 5 percent of its GDP on health services—a proportion much larger than that of other countries with similar incomes—but the health of its people is below average. In Sri Lanka and the state of Kerala in India, however, the very good record of meeting basic needs is not the result of particularly large public expenditure on social services. Sri Lanka's total expenditure on social programs, including rice subsidies, averaged 11 percent of GDP in the 1960s. Kerala spends less on health than many other Indian states do.

Developing countries as a group already spend large sums on health and education and have ambitious plans for the extension of water and sanitation services. In many developing countries educational expenditure per head has doubled during the past twenty-five years, a growth rate twice or three times that of GDP. Education typically accounts for 4 percent of GDP and for 18 to 25 percent of the budget. Most developing countries have publicly financed health care systems and programs of investment in sanitation, water supply, and health education. Fragmentary evidence suggests that public expenditure on health services amounts to 1 to 3 percent of GDP, and total public and private expenditure is 6 to 10 percent of GDP. Additional sums are spent on such health-related activities as family planning, water supply, and sanitation. There thus appears to be scope for reforms within the present totals of expenditure.

Compared with education and health, nutrition and the production of food for domestic consumption have been neglected by many developing countries. Paradoxically, the rich countries with food surpluses have tended to tax poor food consumers to subsidize rich farmers, while the developing countries suffering from food shortages have tended to tax poor farmers to subsidize some relatively well-off urban consumers. These tendencies, which run counter to need, are explained by the power structures. With some exceptions, little attention has been paid to the needs of those suffering from persistent malnutrition, even in countries that could have afforded it.

A basic needs orientation would call for a redistribution of public services to different beneficiaries, a change in the nature of the services, an improvement in their efficiency, and the adoption of an integrated approach. The redesign of the public services from urban to rural, from middle class to deprived groups, from sophisticated to simple, with greater emphasis on the needs of women and small children, is mainly constrained not by money but by political inhibitions and administrative and institutional obstacles.

Sectoral Linkages and Priorities

As has been shown repeatedly, especially in chapter 2, there are strong linkages and complementarities between the supply of various basic needs goods and services. This section adds some specific experiences to the earlier, more general discussion.

Malnutrition makes people more susceptible to disease and to fatalities from disease. In Mali the high death rate among children who have contracted measles is more accurately attributable to its fatal combination with malnutrition, diarrhea, and often malaria. In Recife and parts of Saõ Paulo State in Brazil 50 to 70 percent of all deaths of children under five years old were nutrition-related and an even higher proportion for those under one year; 50 to 70 percent of all deaths from infections and parasitic diseases also had nutrition deficiency as a related cause. In Indonesia specific nutritional deficiencies are responsible for some major diseases: vitamin A deficiency causes eye lesions and blindness; iodine deficiency, goiter and cretinism. Malnutrition among women leads to fatigue (and less attention to household health and nutrition practices), low birth weights of their babies, and malnourishment among breast-fed infants.

Malnutrition, in turn, is partly the result of chronic ill health. A study in the Gambia showed that diarrhea and vomiting, together with other serious infections, appeared to be common causes of the clinical deterioration of nutritional status. Among children less than five years old nutritional status was found to depend primarily on the level of infection, and only secondarily on diet. Parasites in the stomach prevent food absorption, and when they are eliminated the same amount of food gives more nourishment.

Poor sanitation and unsafe water spread many infectious diseases. But in Sri Lanka teaching people when to boil the water substitutes for safe water, which is not widely provided. In Mali,

Somalia, and the Gambia teaching better weaning practices affects health and nutrition. If people learn to provide food and liquids during measles and liquids during diarrhea, the recovery rates improve. If education affects health through its impact on food preparation and personal hygiene, health and nutrition in turn affect education. The health and nutritional status of people affects their willingness and capacity to learn. Malnutrition in infants can permanently affect their mental capacity.

A study in the Gambia noted that, in the absence of effective preventive health care, curative health services are nearly useless, since reinfection normally occurs soon after the patient has been released. Studies in Brazil and Sri Lanka found that female education progressively reduces fertility. The same is true of female participation in the labor force.

Linkages are important not only in increasing the effectiveness but also in reducing the costs of programs. It is now generally agreed that nutrition, family planning, and health care are best delivered together in an integrated program, rather than separately. Not only does an integrated program have a greater effect on population growth, nutrition, and health, it does so at less cost.[1] Water supply, nutrition, and health are cheaper if they are coordinated than if they are supplied by separate government agencies.

In some cases, however, a concentrated attack has value. Benor describes an agricultural extension service in which many field-level extension workers had been made responsible for all aspects of rural development, including health, nutrition, and family planning, as well as for regulatory work, procurement, and the collection of statistics.[2] This might have been justified on grounds of linkages and cost savings, but it was clearly too much for anyone to do, especially poorly paid and inadequately trained

1. B. F. Johnston and A. J. Meyer, "Nutrition, Health and Population in Strategies for Rural Development," *Economic Development and Cultural Change*, vol. 26, no. 1 (1977), pp. 1-23; and B. F. Johnston and William Clark, "Food, Health and Population: Policy Analysis and Development Priorities in Low-Income Countries," Working Paper no. 79-52 (Laxenburg, Austria: International Institute for Applied Systems Analysis, 1979).

2. Daniel Benor and James Q. Harrison, "Agricultural Extension: The Training and Visit System" (Washington, D.C.: World Bank, May 1977; processed).

men. Both the agricultural and the other duties were poorly performed. Benor's approach was to concentrate the work and time of extension personnel exclusively on agricultural extension work, with a single and clear line of command (not split among several authorities), clear specification of duties, and close supervision. The success of this method illustrates the value of a concentrated attack.

The manifold linkages among sectors, with respect to both impact and costs, have led some observers to conclude that a basic needs approach requires multisectoral integrated projects. But most national governments and international organizations tend to be structured along sectoral lines. In some cases, it may be preferable to establish sectoral collaboration through links between different projects rather than attempting an integrated project.

The interdependence among sectors raises the question of sectoral priorities: Must all the outputs for meeting basic needs be provided simultaneously—which would impose impossible administrative and financial costs in many countries—or can sensible sectoral priorities be established? Whatever the resource situation, a rational basic needs program should take into account the interactions between sectors. At this stage too little is known about the relationships to come to a definite conclusion about priorities and linkages, but there is enough evidence for some suggestions.

The causal linkages described point to education, for example, and especially female education, as a likely priority area. Even without additional output from other sectors, extra female education may improve nutrition and health practices, reduce fertility, and improve primary education. But without education improved sanitation and clean water are likely to be ineffective. Education can substitute for such improvements, as it appears to do in Sri Lanka where high life expectancy was achieved while only 20 percent of the people had access to safe water. In contrast, in Egypt more than two-thirds of the population have access to safe water, yet child mortality rates remain high.

Although improvements in nutrition are critical to improved health, increases in food supply alone will not be sufficient to improve nutrition. Much depends on the distribution of food among and within families, which in turn depends on the distribution of purchasing power, the relative price of the various foods, and the spending patterns of families. Aggregate food supply is in excess of requirements in Cuba, Brazil, Indonesia, the Gambia, and Egypt. There does not appear to be any malnutrition in Cuba. But 37 percent of Brazilian children were estimated to be suffering from first degree malnutrition and 20 percent from second degree malnutrition; in Indonesia 20 to 30 percent of the children were shown to be malnourished according to a survey of heights and weights; in the Gambia the nutritional status of rural women and children under five years old is deficient, and according to the studies of the British Medical Research Council the weight of one-year-olds was only 75 percent that of the international standard; in Egypt chronic malnutrition is widespread in rural areas where one quarter of the children are stunted. In contrast, in Sri Lanka, with a significantly lower supply of calories per head, a survey in 1969–70 showed that only 25 percent of the population earning less than 400 rupees a month consumed less than 2,200 calories a day, and only 5 percent less than 1,900 calories. Child mortality rates correspond closely to rates of malnutrition.

Although health is a major objective of the basic needs approach, the evidence here suggests that health services, as conventionally defined, may not be an important input. Curative health services of a Western type are rendered more or less useless in the absence of the other conditions for improving health. For example, in a village in the Gambia, the British Medical Research Council provided specific curative treatment to each child in need. There was only a small difference in child mortality between this village and an untreated control village.

Much depends on the content of the particular sectoral output. For example, the content (what is taught) and method (learning by rote or learning to think) of education are clearly important in determining its effects. The health sector may be largely confined to curative medicine or it may be extended to include a good deal of health education and nutrition.

Several country studies provide some insights into sectoral linkages and priorities, the causal processes at work, and therefore the correct phasing of various interventions. But it is difficult to know whether the results can be generalized from one country to others. Hicks used data from a large number of countries to see whether there are any systematic relationships across countries between achievements in meeting basic needs—defined in terms of life expectancy—and the performance of various indicators of basic needs inputs.[3] The inputs examined include income per head, primary school enrollment, the ratio of female enrollment to total enrollment, access to clean water, availability of doctors and nurses, level of nutrition, public consumption as a proportion of GDP, the degree of urbanization, and the income share of the poorest 40 percent of the population. The data were analyzed in a variety of ways, which in some cases led to conflicting conclusions, but it was fairly firmly established that

—Of the familiar inputs for meeting basic needs, primary education consistently appears to be the most important according to all the measures devised to test relative importance.

—Nutrition and health care seem to be of significance, but less so than education, while water supply is of low priority.

—The distribution of income (measured by the share of the poorest 40 percent) appears to be an important additional factor influencing basic needs, as well as the ratio of female to total primary school enrollment.

—The size of the public sector and the level of urbanization do not seem to be related to basic needs fulfillment.

Naturally, all these conclusions need appropriate qualifications. They are based on inexact and perhaps inadequate measures of basic needs inputs and outputs, and it is difficult to separate cause from effect. The consistent power of education (literacy) is, however, impressive in explaining variations in life expectancy. Broadly, the priorities suggested by analysis of the country experience are borne out by the cross-country statistical

3. Norman L. Hicks, "Sector Priorities in Meeting Basic Needs: Some Statistical Evidence" (Washington, D.C.: World Bank, 1979; processed). Other econometric work confirms these findings.

exercise. But basic needs can be met in a variety of ways—there are no iron laws that must be followed—as shown by examples of countries that deviate from what would be expected at their income level. Tanzania does extremely well for a country of its income level in terms of literacy and water supply, but does not rank high in terms of life expectancy. In fact, its actual life expectancy of 45 is about that expected for its income level (46), and roughly similar to such countries as Zambia and the Ivory Coast, which have much lower literacy rates.[4] Tanzania illustrates the point that despite the generally high association between education and life expectancy, not all countries that have done well in education (as measured by literacy) have necessarily done well on life expectancy. One possible explanation is that Tanzania's gains in education have come recently, and there may be a lag with respect to their impact on life expectancy.

Another interesting case is Egypt, which comes near or at the top of the list of countries doing above average in water supply, calorie supply, and health care. Its life expectancy of 53, however, is only slightly above its expected value of 49. The disappointing performance on basic needs might, in part, be explained by the lack of substantial progress in education; literacy in Egypt is estimated to be 40 percent, only slightly above the expected level of 39. The case of Egypt appears to confirm the importance of education in meeting basic needs.

Women and the roles they are permitted to play are important for meeting basic needs. Whereas in rich countries the life expectancy of women is higher than that of men, in many developing countries it is lower. More than half of all women suffer from anemia, and in some poor countries their health is worsening. Strategies that improve the education, income, and access to basic needs of women may be more productive than other approaches because of the role of women in child care, food preparation, and education in the home. One study found that an additional year of schooling of the mother was associated with

---

4. The World Bank, *World Development Report, 1980* (New York: Oxford University Press, 1980), however, shows a life expectancy for Tanzania in 1978 of 51, substantially above the worldwide norm. Education appears to have contributed to this success.

nine fewer infant and child deaths per thousand, even after allowance was made for the fact that more educated mothers live in urban areas where infant and child mortality is lower. Nutrition and education programs for children are much more effective if they are directed at the women in the family than at the individual child. Water supply projects provide safe water, but improper sanitation in the household can quickly diminish the potential health benefits. The greater benefit of water supply projects may, in fact, be in reducing the work load of women, who sometimes spend as much as half their time hauling water, a fact rarely taken into account in cost-benefit analysis, just as national income accountants neglect the contribution of women in the household. Women also spend much time gathering firewood, walking farther afield as forests are cut down. The provision of alternative fuel would not only check deforestation but also give women more time for education, family care, and political participation. Setting up day-care centers for children frees women's time, gives older girls a chance to stay at school instead of looking after younger siblings at home, and improves the nutrition of children.

Almost all countries that have done well in meeting basic needs have also done well in making primary education available to women (or at least in reducing the bias favoring boys). The reverse, however, is not necessarily true. This suggests that female education is necessary but no guarantee of progress in meeting basic needs. Studies further indicate that improving the employment and productivity of women can have an important effect on meeting basic needs, since women spend a larger share of their incomes on food and health care than do men.

The most difficult group to reach are the poorest 20 percent, the unemployables, the old, disabled, infirm, and sick. Not only are their incomes very low but they also lack access to public services. Provisions intended for them are often diverted to benefit less needy groups. Of course, they constitute a problem also for much more advanced countries, and perhaps only the Scandinavian countries have succeeded in meeting their basic needs.

It has been customary to construct alternative scenarios and to derive from them the number of poor in the year 2000. On the most optimistic assumptions about growth in the industrial countries, about the expansion of aid, loans, and trade, and about the price of energy, the World Bank arrives at 470 million or 13 percent "absolute poor."[5] The base scenario yields 600 million and the pessimistic scenario 710 million.

The optimistic scenario is based on certain assumptions about the links between income growth and income distribution. In line with historical trends, it is assumed that 75 percent of the increases in income would accrue to the top 40 percent of income recipients, and that with strong redistributive policies the share of this group might be reduced to 60 percent. If these assumptions are combined with the rapid growth of the optimistic scenario, the figure can be brought down to between 300 million and 350 million, or less than 10 percent of the population of developing countries. If such improvements in the incomes of the poor reduce fertility rates, the number in absolute poverty would be still lower. Even on the most optimistic assumptions, however, absolute poverty cannot be eliminated by the year 2000.

To eliminate the worst aspects of poverty by the year 2000, a basic needs approach looks deeper than the aggregate income figures and their distribution by deciles and, by more selective and precisely targeted measures, seeks to fulfill basic needs in a shorter period. In this approach poverty is defined not by income, poverty lines, and deciles of the income distribution, but as the inability of identifiable groups of human beings to meet certain basic human needs. Poverty is characterized by hunger and malnutrition, by ill health, and by the lack of education, safe water, sanitation, or decent shelter. A vital task in the elimination of poverty is thus to secure the access of the poor to these goods and services.

The belief that the fulfillment of basic needs is possible earlier than indicated by income projections rests on several pieces of

5. *World Development Report, 1979* (New York: Oxford University Press, 1979).

evidence. First, a comparison of basic needs indicators such as life expectancy and literacy rates with national income per head shows that, despite a general correlation between income and meeting basic needs, there are important exceptions. Critical levels of income per head, as conventionally defined by poverty lines, are neither necessary nor sufficient for meeting basic needs. The objective can be achieved, without excessive costs, at income levels considerably below those indicated by a poverty-line approach based on income growth and the Kuznets curve. This approach relates income distribution to income per head and suggests that at the early phases of development distribution tends to get more unequal.

Second, the necessary changes have been implemented by a wide variety of political regimes in areas of different sizes, histories, and traditions. Among them are market economies such as Taiwan and South Korea, mixed economies such as Sri Lanka, centrally planned economies such as China and Cuba, and decentralized planned economies such as Yugoslavia. What they have in common is a fairly equal distribution of land, a degree of decentralization of decisionmaking with adequate central support, and attention to what goes on within the household, particularly to the role of women.

Third, a concerted attack on several factors simultaneously, combined with the correct phasing, can substantially improve the well-being of the poor and reduce costs. Relatively low-cost improvements in education, nutrition, and health considerably reduce the need for large and expensive investments in shelter, water supply, and sanitation.

Fourth, there is much scope for reallocating expenditure in favor of the poor both within the private and the public sectors and from the private to the public sector, without mobilizing additional resources. This may run into political obstacles and psychological inhibitions, but it is not constrained by a lack of resources.

Fifth, the basic needs approach throws important new light on narrowing the gap between rich and poor countries. In the past, this gap has usually been defined in terms of relative income per head. It is very doubtful whether closing the income gap in the near future is either desirable or possible. But closing the gap in terms of fulfilling basic needs as shown by such indicators as life expectancy, literacy rates, or nutrition levels is more desirable, feasible, and worthy of effort in international cooperation. Life expectancy is biologically bounded somewhere around seventy years. Literacy rates cannot be more than 100 percent. Adequate nutrition levels can be exceeded. Therefore closing the basic needs gap is a more sensible and appealing objective than closing the income gap, and it should mobilize national and international support.

The experience of a great variety of countries and sectoral programs teaches that far more progress can be made toward the fulfillment of basic needs by the year 2000 than is suggested by the conventional economic approach based on income growth and poverty lines. If it is physically and technically possible to meet the basic needs of the world population within the next generation, let us exercise our social imagination, mobilize the political base, and improve our political and organizational management to do so. With a strong enough national and international commitment and the mobilization of underutilized human resources, it is not unrealistic to aim at eliminating the worst aspects of poverty within a generation.

8

The Role of the International Community

THE BASIC NEEDS CONCEPT has entered the North-South dialogue, and misconceptions have grown around it. The North-South dialogue is largely concerned with the New International Economic Order (NIEO), a term that arose from the United Nations declaration of May 1974 and gave rise to several related statements by the developing countries in the late 1970s. These statements called for a reconstruction of the existing international economic system in the areas of trade, finance, technology transfer, and national sovereignty as a means to improve development prospects in the developing countries, narrow disparities in income between rich and poor countries, and give the developing countries more control over their own destinies.

The relations between the basic needs approach and the NIEO can be discussed at several levels. At the level of logic the discussion would find that the concept of the NIEO is concerned with international issues, whereas the concept of basic needs concerns domestic issues. In spite of apparent inconsistencies, the concepts are complementary: if the NIEO would generate more resources for the developing countries, this could contribute to the satisfaction of basic needs; and the objective of meeting basic needs can be seen to mobilize support for international cooperation. Acceptance of the NIEO derives much of its force from a united effort to eradicate poverty.

At the level of economics it would have to be shown how the various NIEO measures contribute to meeting basic needs: which countries and which groups within countries would benefit from which provisions and under what conditions. One would want to know how government revenue from taxation or aid receipts is spent, who benefits from trade liberalization, from commodity schemes, and from debt relief. And one would investigate how domestic efforts to eradicate poverty can be internationally supported.

At the level of international politics the motives, fears, and apprehensions of the negotiating partners need to be analyzed and ways devised to clarify issues and to design institutions and procedures that would eliminate these fears. Finally, at the level of domestic interest groups, one would wish to examine the resistance of vested interests to the implementation of basic needs approaches and the NIEO. To what extent do the objections of the international negotiators reflect the obstacles and inhibitions of particular groups in the South which resist doing more for the poor, or masked opposition by vested interests in the North which are trying to protect themselves?

The Logic

On superficial inspection there appears to be a conflict between the two concepts. The NIEO aims at revising the rules of international economic relations between nations and is the particular concern of governments, whereas the basic needs approach considers the needs of individuals and households. The NIEO deals with issues such as commodity price stabilization and support, indexation, the Common Fund, the Integrated Commodity Program, debt relief, the Special Drawing Rights (SDR) link,[1] trade liberalization, trade preferences, technology transfer, and transnational firms, whereas basic needs refers to food, water, health, education, and shelter. The NIEO aims at unconditional, automatic or semiautomatic, concealed transfers of resources (or

1. The Common Fund and the Integrated Commodity Program aim to stabilize the prices of a group of primary products, mainly exported by the developing countries, and thereby achieve higher and more stable export receipts. The SDR link aims at linking the issue of new Special Drawing Rights, the international reserve asset, with additional aid to developing countries.

at correcting past reverse transfers), whereas the basic needs approach is highly selective, aiming directly at the alleviation of deprivation of particular groups. The NIEO would eliminate conditions imposed on resource transfers; a basic needs approach would wish to make transfers conditional on their reaching the poor. The schemes proposed in the NIEO are likely to benefit the middle-income countries and some very small (already relatively overaided) countries, in whose economies foreign trade plays an important part, rather than the large, poor countries of Asia; within these small and middle-income countries, the proposed schemes may benefit the middle- and higher-income groups, such as exporting industrialists (possibly multinational corporations), farmers with large holdings, plantation owners, and banks, rather than the urban and rural poor.

But the apparent logical conflict between basic needs and the NIEO can be avoided. The differences between the two approaches point to the need to advance on both fronts simultaneously. The NIEO is concerned with formulating a framework of institutions, processes, and rules that would correct what developing countries regard as the present bias against them. This bias is thought to be evident in the structure of certain markets, where a few large and powerful buyers confront many weak, competing sellers, in the tariff structures and the nature of vertically integrated firms that discriminate against processing in developing countries, in restricted access to capital markets and to knowledge, in the present patent law and patent conventions, in the thrust of research and development, and the nature of modern technology, in the power of the transnational corporations, in shipping, and in international monetary arrangements. A correction in the direction of a more balanced distribution of power would enable developing countries to become less dependent and more self-reliant. But the NIEO by itself would be no guarantee that the governments of the developing countries would use their new power to meet the needs of their poor. The basic needs approach, by focusing on the goods and services needed by deprived people, households, and communities, highlights the importance of the needs of individual human beings.

A basic needs program that does not build on the self-reliance and self-help of governments and countries is in danger of degenerating into a global charity program and can be counterproductive by pauperizing the poor. A NIEO that is not committed to meeting basic needs is liable to transfer resources from the poor in rich countries to the rich in poor countries.

It is easy to envisage a situation in which the benefits of international assistance for basic needs are more than wiped out by an unreformed international order: by protectionist trade and foreign investment, by transfer pricing practices of multinationals, by the unemployment generated by inappropriate technology, or by restrictive monetary policies. The global commitment to basic needs makes sense only in an international order in which all international policies other than aid—trade, foreign investment, technology transfer, movement of professionals, money—are not detrimental to a self-reliant strategy of meeting basic needs. Insofar as the NIEO makes more resources available to the developing countries, basic needs can be met sooner.

The situation is similar in some respects to the rise of trade unions in nineteenth-century England. Those concerned with the fate of the poor remained relatively ineffective until the poor were permitted by law to organize themselves, bargain collectively, strike, and have their funds protected. There has, however, always been the danger that trade unions would turn into another powerful estate, less concerned with the fate of the poor than with protecting the privileges of a labor aristocracy. And there is the possibility that the strong unions will reap gains at the expense of the weaker ones and the unorganized workers.

The NIEO calls for a revision of the rules and institutions regulating the relations between sovereign nations, and of the power relations behind them, and meeting basic needs is one important objective which this framework should serve. There are those who maintain that integration into any international economic order dominated by advanced capitalist economies is inconsistent with meeting the basic needs of the poor. Pointing to the example of China, until recently, they advocate "delinking," to insulate their society or group of like-minded societies from the detrimental impulses propagated by the international system. Policies derived from such a view of the world order do not, of course, depend on wringing concessions from rich countries, but can be pursued by unilateral action.

Other analysts, who think the international system has benefits to offer if the rules are reformulated and the power relations recast, will opt not for complete delinking, but for restructuring. Restructuring has implications for domestic policies in both developed and developing countries and for international policies. If the industrialized countries really want to help the developing countries pursue a basic needs approach, they must assist their own workers to shift from labor-intensive industries to better, more remunerative employment and make room for labor-intensive imports, which will generate employment and income for the poor in the low-income countries. The developing countries will in turn use the receipts from their exports to import capital-intensive products, such as fertilizer, steel, synthetic fibers, and technology-intensive products from the industrialized countries, thus enabling their workers' earnings to increase also.

The Economics

In principle, the concepts of the NIEO and basic needs are complementary. But much would depend, of course, on which measures of the NIEO are adopted and on how they are implemented. There is remarkably little research on the effect of the various NIEO proposals on local poverty groups. Some work has been done on the country distribution of commodity schemes and trade liberalization, but hardly any on how they would affect domestic income distribution and alleviate poverty. A commodity program that restricts the production of small farms in order to raise prices would benefit the large plantation owners, but it would benefit small-scale farmers if the output of large producers were restricted. Debt relief may benefit banks in industrial countries, the SDR link treasuries. The distribution of the benefits from trade liberalization would depend on who exports the

additional products, at what remuneration, how they are produced, and so forth. Even if the rich benefit in the first round,
taxation would make redistribution possible. But equally, if the
poor benefit in the first round, redistribution upward may take
place later. The largest benefits of the NIEO would come if
industrial countries met the goal of allocating 0.7 percent of their
GNP to development assistance, and the link between this
achievement and basic needs would depend on how governments spend aid funds.

If the emphasis of the NIEO is on directing concessional finance
to the poorest countries with governments determined to tackle
poverty, the impact on basic needs would be strong. If, however, the emphasis is on improving market access and the terms
for technology transfer, middle-income countries and households would be favored. Many NIEO measures would increase
government revenues, whether directly as in the case of official
development assistance, or indirectly through taxation of extra
profits and incomes. If the governments adopt the appropriate
policies, these measures will be favorable to meeting basic needs.
The economics of the relation between the NIEO and basic needs
is at the heart of the matter, and remarkably little thought has
been given to ways in which possible conflicts can be avoided.

Many NIEO proposals are intended to speed up industrialization. Industrialization is entirely compatible with meeting basic
needs, but it does not inevitably do so.[2] Much depends on
whether the industrialization is capital intensive or labor intensive, and on the kinds of product produced for the domestic
market.

The ideal combination would be for a national government to
commit itself to meeting the basic needs of its people—for example, by a campaign to eliminate hunger and malnutrition—and
for the international community to commit additional financial
and technical assistance to such a program. As indicated in the
earlier discussion of nutrition, the eradication of hunger and

---

2. Ajit Singh, "The 'Basic Needs' Approach to Development vs. the New International Economic Order: The Significance of Third World Industrialization," *World Development*, vol. 7, no. 6 (June 1979), pp. 585–606.

malnutrition within ten to twenty years calls for food subsidies and direct distribution, and selective schemes that provide for food entitlement are the most effective. It would be in the spirit of the unity of the New International Economic Order and the basic needs approach if there were an international initiative to mobilize support for a national campaign of this kind. The support would include financial assistance, aid in kind through food shipments, technical assistance in the management of the program and its integration into development policies, assistance in monitoring the program, and the regular assessment of assistance needs and donor performance. Such a scheme would provide food at lower prices to poor consumers in developing countries, and at the same time it would stimulate the production of more food. Such an initiative would not reduce the need for domestic and international measures to create employment, reduce gross inequalities, and accelerate economic growth. But it would offer international support to countries that are serious about eradicating hunger.

The International Politics

"Basic needs" (like "appropriate technology") has fallen into disrepute in the North-South dialogue. At international meetings delegates from the developing countries have vehemently rejected the basic needs concept. There has been concern over the potential hypocrisy of such a strategy and suspicion about the intentions of aid-giving governments and international agencies. This concern and suspicion are justified because some donors have misinterpreted and abused the concept. Donor abuses and recipient fears have taken the following forms:

1. A basic needs approach has been interpreted as a substitute for growth, modernization, industrialization, and self-reliance. Industrialization has brought wealth and power to the North, and it is felt that the rich now wish to prevent the developing countries from following the same path.
2. The slogan of basic needs has been used to justify the reduction of foreign aid to the poorest countries because of their lack of projects and of "absorptive capacity."

3. Middle-income countries have feared that with the basic needs approach the rich nations will reduce aid to them on the pretext of concentrating on the poorest countries.

4. A basic needs approach can be used to slow down or prevent the rapid growth of manufactured exports from the developing countries and can serve as a thinly disguised protectionist device of the established, inefficient manufacturing lobbies.

5. The introduction of basic needs criteria may pave the way for donors to violate national sovereignty and interfere in the autonomous setting of development priorities.

6. In addition, the slogan can be used to cloak the introduction of irrelevant or controversial political, social, or economic criteria of performance. Both this point and the one preceding raise the objection of unacceptable intrusiveness.

7. Above all, it is felt that the basic needs approach has been used as a diversionary tactic to draw attention from the New International Economic Order.

At the heart of this debate lies the controversy over whether poverty in the midst of global plenty is the result of intended or unintended exploitation or neglect on the part of the rich countries and the rules of the international system, or whether it is the result of the power structure, attitudes, institutions, and policies of the developing countries.

Two points are worth noting. First, governments of developing countries have many objectives in addition to meeting basic needs. These include achieving military goals, independence, or Northern style industrialization; meeting non–basic needs of the upper classes; in some cases establishing a democratic government in which the nonpoor have a majority, and so forth. Second, in spite of the hostility to the basic needs concept in international discussions, this and similar objectives figure prominently in national planning and policymaking.[3]

For instance, the 1979–83 development plan for Kenya states that the "alleviation of poverty is not only an objective in our

3. See Norman L. Hicks, "Basic Needs and the New International Economic Order," Background Paper for *World Development Report, 1980* (Washington, D.C.: World Bank, 1979; processed).

development efforts, it is also a major instrument for ensuring that our development is rapid, stable and sustainable . . . Improvements of the well-being of the people remain our dominant aim."[4] Similarly, the Philippine 1978–82 development plan indicates that "the conquest of mass poverty becomes the immediate, fundamental goal of Philippine development." Development over the next decade "will be a massive effort to provide for the basic needs of the majority of the population."[5]

India's new draft plan for 1978–83 suggests "what matters is not the precise rate of increase in the national product that is achieved in five or ten years, but whether we can ensure within a specified time frame a measurable increase in the welfare of the millions of poor."[6] The three principal objectives of this plan are listed as the removal of unemployment and underemployment, the rise in the standard of living of the poor, and the provision by the state of certain basic needs, namely, drinking water, literacy, elementary education, health care, rural roads, rural housing, and minimum services in urban slums. The plan puts forward a revised "Minimum Needs Program," which substantially increases allocations for water supply, basic education, rural roads, and other identified basic needs. At the same time, at a meeting of the U.N. Committee of the Whole, the Indian delegate indicated that his government was "strongly against any attempt to direct the attention of the international community to alternative approaches to development cooperation, such as the basic needs approach."[7]

The Sixth Plan of Nepal (1980–85) lists as its first two objectives the "gradual elimination of absolute poverty through employment opportunities" and the "fulfillment of minimum basic needs." Meeting basic needs is seen as a way to "enhance the efficiency and productivity" of low-income groups in backward areas. These minimum needs are listed as being "potable water,

4. Government of Kenya, *Development Plan, 1979 to 1983*, pp. ii–iii.
5. Government of the Philippines, *Five Year Philippine Development Plan, 1978–82*, p. 1-1.
6. Government of India, Planning Commission, *Draft Five Year Plan, 1978–83*, vol. 1, p. 8.
7. U.N. General Assembly, A/AC. 191/21, April 28, 1978, p. 4.

minimum health care, primary and skill-oriented education, family planning and maternity and child-health care services, irrigation facilities," as well as basic transport and agricultural extension services.[8] How these principles will be carried into the final plan document and its resource allocations, however, is not yet clear.

South Korea is known as a country that has already made substantial progress on basic needs. Yet Korea's Fourth Plan (1977–82) significantly increased allocations for social development while maintaining a heavy emphasis on industrial development and export-led growth. In Indonesia, the Third Plan (1979–84) states its "essential goals" are "to raise the living standards and levels of knowledge of the Indonesian people, to strive for a more equitable and just distribution of welfare." Equitable distribution is an objective in providing "access to means of fulfilling basic human needs, especially food, clothing and shelter" as well as access to health and educational facilities, jobs, and incomes, and in promoting regional development.[9]

Since 1975, Ethiopia has made significant progress in providing the poor with basic health services, primary education, and the like. While the government does not use the term "basic needs," its annual plan reveals its long-term objectives to be "raising the standard of living of the broad masses of the people, abolishing poverty, ignorance, disease and unemployment." Standards of living will be increased "through an adequate provision of the daily necessities such as food, grain, clothing, etc."[10]

Not all countries have made an explicit shift to a basic needs policy. In Tunisia the new five-year plan (Fifth Plan of Economic and Social Development) increases the emphasis on employment and income distribution, but does not give priority to a basic needs strategy. The 1976–80 plan for Malaysia emphasizes the

8. Nepal, National Planning Commission Secretariat, *Basic Principles of Sixth Plan, 1980–85* (Katmandu, April 1979), pp. 17-19.

9. Government of Indonesia, *Repelita III: The Third Five Year Development Plan, 1979–84* (Jakarta, 1979; English translation), p. 2.

10. Provisional Military Government of Socialist Ethiopia, *First Year Programme of the National Revolutionary Development Campaign* (May 1979), pp. 13 and 10.

alleviation of poverty by increasing productivity, reducing population pressure, and increasing employment, as well as by providing essential services such as water supply, education, and electricity. But the Malaysian plan was drafted largely before "basic needs" had become a banner. Many countries, such as Sri Lanka, Burma, Tanzania, Madagascar, and Algeria, have already made a heavy commitment to social development and therefore have not felt the need to shift priorities. In many new plans still being formulated, such as those for Mexico, Niger, and Afghanistan, more emphasis is likely to be placed on basic needs, income distribution, and employment issues. In Egypt, past development efforts have given high priority to social development, but this has been centered principally on urban areas. The new development plan for Egypt shifts the allocation of resources to the rural areas and increases the amount of rural participation in planning decisions. In some countries (Sudan, Morocco, Peru), plans to expand social sector expenditures and poverty-oriented programs have been delayed because of resource constraints. In still other countries (Ivory Coast, Colombia), no shift in development priorities appears probable. On the whole, however, a large number of countries have oriented their development strategies more toward alleviating poverty and meeting basic needs, or are about to do so.

Rhetoric embodied in development plans does not necessarily mean a serious commitment. In many cases, however, the new plans reviewed here show increased allocations for the social sectors in support of a basic needs strategy. This is true specifically of South Korea, Indonesia, Kenya, Malaysia, and the Philippines. In the Philippines social sector expenditures will increase from 23.5 percent of total expenditures in 1977 to 28.1 percent in 1982, while in Kenya the development budget plan increases their share from 21.7 percent (FY1974–78) to 27.4 percent (FY1979–83). In India the allocations for the social sectors actually decline as a share of the total development expenditures while the commitment to basic needs is increased.

Commitment to basic needs cannot be measured by the total resource allocation to the social sectors, however, since much can be accomplished by a reallocation within the sectors. This suggests that for those countries already allocating significant resources to the social sectors, reallocation can be used to meet basic needs without reducing investment in non–basic needs activities or decreasing non–basic needs consumption. A change in plan allocations does not, of course, necessarily mean that resources will eventually find their way into these sectors. Historically, the social sectors have generally been considered "soft" and prime candidates for reductions in allocations in times of financial austerity. But there is growing recognition of the political risks involved in continuing to ignore the basic needs of the majority of a country's population, while continuing to provide services for the urban elite.

It is therefore evident that the developing countries' opposition to the basic needs approach, at least in their declarations, is not so stark as it is often made out to be.[11] Planning and treasury officials speak with a different voice and from a different tradition and training from those of foreign office officials, and the objections may be more to the international forums than to the substance of the discussions. It is fairly clear, however, that the domestic rhetoric is not always matched by a willingness to implement the declarations.

The Seven Suspicions

Let us return to the seven suspicions and look briefly at each of them.

11. Basic needs "peaked in the nearly unanimous adoption at the ILO's World Employment Conference in 1976 (without major dissent by any developing country delegation) of a recommendation that a basic needs strategy be made central to the international as well as domestic aspects of development promotion. Yet scarcely had the members of DAC, little more than a year later, gone to the rather unusual length of themselves adopting a thoughtful but (in its deference to host governments' priorities and prerogatives) guarded endorsement of just such a focus, when it became the official policy of the '77' to attack the basic needs approach root and branch—as diversionary and unacceptably intrusive—in most international fora." (*Development Co-operation, 1979 Review*, Report by the Chairman of the Development Assistance Committee [DAC] of the Organisation for Economic Co-operation and Development, November 1979, p. 51.)

1. Meeting basic human needs, it was argued in chapter 5, need not be at the expense of growth; on the contrary, growth is an indispensable prerequisite (or, rather, result), though it is composed and distributed differently than the dualistic and concentrated growth that has failed to benefit the poor. Nor does it follow that a basic needs approach must confine itself to low or intermediate technology. Some highly modern technology may be required, such as satellites for aerial photography and remote sensing. Private and public investment and administrative resources have to be redirected from high-income to low-income sectors so as to raise the productivity and incomes of the latter, in the service of both efficiency and equity; the work of the poor has to be made more remunerative; public services have to be radically redesigned so as to cover more people more cheaply; and the private incomes of the poor have to be adequate to give them access to public services. All this cannot be done without modernization, industrialization, and economic growth.

2. A global commitment to meeting basic needs requires more, not fewer, international resources. And international cooperation for basic needs performance is practical only if the international community provides additional resources. Provisional estimates indicate that a basic needs program to provide minimum acceptable diets, safe water, sewerage facilities, public health measures, and basic education and to upgrade existing shelter would call for substantial investment and additional recurrent expenditures. If the OECD countries were to concentrate their effort on the poorest countries and contribute about 50 percent of the additional costs of these programs, this would call for a very large increase in official development assistance (ODA) over twenty years. A figure of $20 thousand million a year at 1976 prices for the 1980–2000 period has been calculated.

In 1978 total ODA flows amounted to more than $22 thousand million a year. Of this, the poorest countries receive only about $10 thousand million. Only a part of this assistance is at present devoted to meeting basic needs. It might be asked why the whole of the assistance should not be switched to what is agreed to be a priority objective, so that additional requirements could be greatly reduced. If, moreover, some ODA now going to middle-income countries could be redirected to the poorest countries, requirements could be further reduced.

Such redirection would, however, be neither desirable nor possible. Middle-income countries have a higher absorptive capacity and tend to show higher returns on resource transfers. They, too, have serious problems of poverty. Moreover, a reallocation of ODA flows is politically much easier if it is done out of incremental flows than if existing flows to some countries have to be cut. The legacy of past commitments and the expectations that they have generated cannot be discarded in a few years.

Substantial additional resources are needed to make a convincing international contribution to basic needs programs in the poorest countries for three reasons. First, twenty years is a very short time for a serious anti-poverty program. It calls for extra effort from both developed and developing countries. The domestic effort—economic, administrative, and political—required from the developing countries is formidable. At the same time, the financial assistance from the developed countries would be gradually raised to average an additional $20 thousand million a year over twenty years. Although this figure seems large, total ODA flows would still be only 0.43 percent of the GNP of the OECD countries in 2000, substantially below the target of 0.7 percent. The acceleration (from the present 0.34 percent of GNP) is certainly within the power of the developed countries, and if the task is to be taken seriously by both sides, an increase of this magnitude appears to be a reasonable basis for mutual reassurance.

The second reason for additional assistance is that the transition from present policies to a basic needs approach creates formidable problems of transition.[12] Investment projects that

12. See the section "Problems of Transition" in chapter 2. A former prime minister of Great Britain reflected: "I experienced the same problem in a rather different way in Ghana in 1971. Its government was asking only for sufficient finance to take clean water, sanitation and lighting to the villages. If it had been able to do this its democratic regime could have achieved sufficient support to face other criticism. As we failed to muster sufficient funds to cover even these basic needs the democratic regime was overthrown by a military coup." (Edward Heath, "The Way to Avoid a Caribbean Crisis," *The* [London] *Times,* March 12, 1980.)

have been started cannot suddenly be terminated. An attempt to switch to a basic needs program while the structure of demand and production has not yet been adapted to it is bound to create unemployment and inflationary pressures and to strain the balance of payments. There might be capital flight and added brain drain as social groups attempt to safeguard their interests and avoid being hurt. There might be strikes from disaffected workers in the organized industrial sector. Unless a government has some reserves to overcome these transitional difficulties, the attempt to embark on a basic needs program might be nipped in the bud.

The third reason for additional assistance is tactical and political. It is well known that the developing countries are suspicious of the basic needs approach, in part because they believe that pious words conceal a desire to reduce development assistance. And there is no doubt that some people in the developed world see the basic needs approach as a cheap option. If the international commitment to meeting basic needs within a short period is to be taken seriously by the developing countries, the contribution by the developed countries must be additional and substantial. The essence of the international dialogue is that both developed and developing countries should reach a basic understanding to meet the human needs of the poor within a reasonable time. Such a dialogue would be a sham if it did not involve substantial additional capital transfers and technical assistance.

3. While the bulk of incremental development aid should be devoted to the poorest countries committed to a basic needs approach, some extra aid should be available for middle-income countries that commit themselves to the eradication of their pockets of poverty. It is an essential feature of the basic needs approach that, because basic needs may be unmet at quite high income levels, adequate income is not enough to eliminate deprivation. Better access to capital markets, more liberal trade opportunities, and loans at commercial interest rates are the appropriate forms in which the international community can contribute to increasing the resources and thereby the ability to meet basic needs in the less poor developing countries.

4. The fourth apprehension is that the basic needs approach would be used to stop or retard the growth of manufactured imports from developing economies. As the examples of Taiwan, South Korea, and Singapore show, labor-intensive exports can be a powerful instrument to create jobs and therefore to combine high growth rates with the fulfillment of basic needs. Growth in the developing countries affects the developed countries in two ways, the balance of which changes over time. It can create additional demand for the developed countries' exports, and it can provide competitive sources of supplies in the home markets of both the developing and the developed countries and in third markets. The change in the balance from the early stages of industrialization, in which the demand for capital goods dominated, to the more recent phase, in which competitive supplies dominate, appears to have contributed to the popularity of basic needs strategies in some donor circles. But an emphasis on agriculture, the rural sector, and labor-intensive industries is not in conflict with export-led industrialization. On the contrary, it is a necessary condition for it.

5. The fifth concern is about the excessive intrusiveness of the basic needs approach. It is possible, however, to combine full sovereignty and autonomy with meeting basic needs. Buffer institutions or buffer processes, acceptable to both recipient and donor countries, would protect the recipients' sovereignty and the donors' wishes by channeling funds in the right direction and by monitoring performance in meeting basic needs. Multilateral institutions are particularly suited for this role. Developing countries themselves could monitor each other's implementation of basic needs programs, financed by industrial countries, as was done in the Marshall Plan for Europe.

6. Similarly, the way to avoid the intrusion of irrelevant criteria into aid transactions is to channel aid through multilateral institutions, in which developing countries are fairly represented, or to institute a system of mutual monitoring by the developing countries.

7. The main fear of the developing countries is that the adoption of a basic needs approach by donors implies sacrificing

certain features of the New International Economic Order, such as larger transfers of resources from the North to the South and reforms in the international distribution of power. The NIEO call for these changes arises from the belief among developing countries that distortions in international markets are stunting their development efforts and limiting their prospects.

Once the apprehensions of the developing countries have been cleared away by insisting on the correct interpretation of the basic needs approach, how is an international basic needs approach to be implemented in a manner consistent with the spirit of the NIEO? On the one hand, the governments of developing countries are anxious to preserve their full sovereignty and autonomy and do not wish to have their priorities laid down for them by donors. They dislike strings attached to aid and close scrutiny of its use. Donors, on the other hand, wish to make sure that their contributions reach the people for whom they are intended.[13] The solution is to strengthen existing institutions and procedures, and create new ones, that are acceptable to both donors and recipients and ensure that international aid reaches the vulnerable groups. Such buffer institutions and buffer processes would respect full national sovereignty while giving priority to meeting basic needs. They would be representative, independent, and genuinely devoted to the goals of international cooperation.

It is clear that only multilateral or extranational institutions can meet these conditions. But reform may be required on several issues. Votes must be distributed in a way that developing countries feel gives them fair representation. The selection, recruitment, and training of members of the international secretariat must transcend narrowly national loyalties and be sensitive to the social and cultural issues in developing countries. Both narrow technocracy and an excessive politicization of issues will have to

13. A. K. Sen has rightly pointed out that, if there is a moral claim of the poor on the rich in the world community, it must be shown that the resources raised by rich countries reach the poor in poor countries, and that not giving such aid (and, for example, reducing taxes) would benefit the poor in the rich countries. ("Ethical Issues in Income Distribution: National and International," paper presented to the symposium on the Past and Prospects of the Economic World Order, Saltsjöbaden, Sweden, August 1978.)

be avoided. It may be thought that this amounts to a prescription for perfection. But international institutions and their secretariats have in some instances approximated these ideal canons. Unless they do, there is little hope of implementing a basic needs approach in the framework of the NIEO.[14]

Vested Interests

Conflict between the NIEO and the basic needs approach can spring from any of four sources: there can be conflict at the definitional level, but I have argued that clarification of the concepts shows them to be complementary. Second, there can be conflict in the economic implications. Here, more research and thought on appropriate policies are needed. Third, there can be conflict at the level of international negotiations because of misinterpretations for political purposes. Fourth, conflict can arise when organized interest groups, in either the developed or the developing countries, resist implementation because they would get hurt. Resistance to the NIEO can come from industrialists in advanced countries who wish the developing countries to refrain from competing with their products and to remain pastoral societies that export primary products. Resistance to the basic needs approach can spring from the ruling classes of developing countries in the absence of the desire to do anything for their poor. The beneficiaries of concentrated and uneven growth are unwilling to share the fruits of this growth with the poor in their own countries. For them, opposition to meeting basic needs and insistence on the NIEO serve as a convenient smoke screen. This is particularly true of some middle-income countries in which total resources would be adequate to meet basic needs, but the extremely unequal income distribution and the interests of the rich stand in the way. Since the world is organized in sovereign nation states, foreign pressures or persuasion may not be very

14. For some imaginative ideas on how to combine international institutions devoted to basic needs with respect for national sovereignty, see Harlan Cleveland, *The Third Try at World Order* (New York: Aspen Institute for Humanistic Studies and World Affairs Council of Philadelphia, 1976).

productive, but there is no reason such regimes should qualify for any of the additional resources made available specifically for meeting the basic needs of the poor.

Negative Responses to a Basic Needs Approach in Rich Countries

The objections to a basic needs approach raised by the developing countries have been discussed at some length, but rich donor countries are by no means universally enthusiastic. Opposition to the implementation of a basic needs approach to development among officials, politicians, and academics in donor countries and agencies can be summarized under the following headings:

1. The approach would sacrifice investment, output, productivity, and growth for the sake of current consumption and welfare transfers, which only rich countries can afford.
2. Donors respond to the requests of developing countries, whose attitude toward the basic needs approach is at best lukewarm; at worst, hostile.
3. There is nothing new except the label; basic needs are already being met under the banner of poverty orientation, employment creation, or rural development.
4. Implementation of a basic needs approach is constrained by political obstacles inside the developing countries, and there is nothing the international community can do about this.
5. The basic needs approach is used as the Trojan horse of communism (Maoism, socialism), and most countries with which the industrialized nations cooperate do not wish to adopt these ideologies and forms of government.
6. The basic needs concept is often interpreted to require state intervention in the market, and the numerous defects of bureaucratic interference are too well known to need rehearsing; consumers are the best judges of their needs, markets are quite efficient instruments of allocation, and the paternalism implied by this concept is unacceptable.

7. Inadequate attention has been paid to the problem of transition; inflation, capital flight, strikes, and other macroeconomic consequences are liable to prevent a government from meeting basic needs.

8. The basic needs approach has no analytical content and is largely rhetoric or polemics; no one can dispute the desirability of the objective, but implementation is either fuzzy or, where spelled out, inefficient, unsuited to achieve the declared objective, and possibly counterproductive.

Brief replies (some of which are more fully discussed in other contexts) would be along the following lines.

1. The first criticism is not valid. The logical precedence of ends over means in no way implies that means can be neglected. On the contrary, to meet basic needs on a sustainable basis calls for considerable investment and growth, although it will be differently composed, distributed, and measured than in the past. Growth is also required to meet the rising standards as income per head grows, and to achieve objectives other than meeting basic needs.

At the same time, the basic needs approach is a way of doing more and doing better with fewer resources: replicable preventive medical services for all, instead of high-cost services for a few; low-cost village primary education for the rural poor instead of high-cost urban tertiary education of the privileged. Economy in the use of existing resources and augmentation of these resources by increasing productivity, reducing fertility, and mobilizing local underutilized resources are important aspects of this approach. (See "The Case for Basic Needs" in chapter 1.)

2. Donors can select for assistance those countries that are themselves eager to embark on a basic needs approach. Even where there is resistance, some solicitation of requests can shift development programs in the direction of greater emphasis on meeting basic needs. Recipient governments are rarely monolithic, and aid and dialogue can support the internal forces that are anxious to meet basic needs within a short time.

3. Although the concept of basic needs is based on a good deal of accumulated experience and knowledge, it does contain some

distinctive and novel features. They can be best summarized as the need to redesign public services to complement improved earning power, to pay more attention to activities inside the household, to initiate a wider range of government interventions, and to place greater emphasis on self-management and the local mobilization of resources. There is also the positive, operational, and concrete emphasis on meeting specific needs of vulnerable groups, which previous, more aggregative and more abstract approaches have tended to neglect.

4. It is true that some of the most severe constraints are political, but these should not be regarded as irremovable. Alliances with reformist groups, encouraged both by the careful selection of countries and by dialogue, can remove some of these obstacles. But politics is not the whole answer. There are gaps in our knowledge and experience, and administrative difficulties in implementing a basic needs approach. Such an approach makes heavy demands on managerial and administrative skills, which are scarce in most developing countries, but the demands are not of the highest order. The breaking of these administrative bottlenecks and the exploration of appropriate technologies and delivery systems are challenges quite distinct from the problem of overcoming political resistance. Even where the political forces have been favorable, basic needs programs have sometimes failed because of organizational defects.

5. It is perfectly true that inequality indexes and poverty measures are lower in socialist than in capitalist countries. Revolutionary land reforms and public ownership of all means of production make it easier to pursue a basic needs strategy (though inequalities of power and access to power are increased by the existence of a centralized bureaucracy). But the success of a number of nonsocialist countries in meeting basic needs suggests that socialism is not a prerequisite for doing so. And, as Cambodia has shown, it certainly does not guarantee that basic needs are met.

6. The question of how much "supply management" in the form of market intervention is necessary should be treated as an empirical one and should be answered pragmatically, not ideologically. The deficiencies of bureaucratic controls are well known. At the same time, market imperfections in the widest

sense have often prevented market responses to private purchasing power, even where this was fairly evenly distributed.

The basic needs concept is not derived from a paternalistic ideology, although it acknowledges that consumers are subject to all kinds of pressures—from advertisers and from their own wish to emulate the consumption patterns of other groups—against which countervailing pressures can legitimately be mobilized. Ultimately, it is the felt needs of human beings in society that should define the content of a basic needs program.

7. Radical reforms that have failed demonstrate the need to give careful thought to the political and economic problems of the transition from a society in which assets, income, and power are unequally distributed and deprivation is widespread to one in which basic needs are met. Disequilibriums in particular markets, inflation, capital flight, brain drain, or disruption of production by disaffected groups are dangers that can frustrate a basic needs approach before it has gone very far. These threats point to the need to work out carefully the macroeconomic implications, both domestic and international, of the transition to basic needs strategies (see the section "Problems of Transition" in chapter 2).

8. The criticism that the basic needs approach lacks analytical content is probably of greater concern to academic economists, who justify their existence by saying the nonobvious, than to people concerned with getting things done. It also happens to be untrue, for meeting basic needs calls for a complex analysis of externalities in cross-sectoral linkages, both to reduce costs and to improve the impact on meeting needs. It is true, however, that some of the most important unsettled issues lie in the area of politics and administration, rather than in economic analysis.

It may, of course, turn out that some of the approaches that are intended to meet basic needs will be inefficient or even counterproductive. "Trickle-up" and "government failure" or "bureaucratic failure" (corresponding in the public sector to "market failure" in the private sector) are bound to occur in delivery systems, and some tradeoffs with more conventional objectives may have to be accepted. But in view of the lack of success of many previous approaches in reaching the deprived, experimentation with new methods should be welcomed.

Appendix

Basic Needs and Human Rights

Is THE SATISFACTION OF BASIC NEEDS a human right? Are minimum levels of nutrition, health, and education among the most fundamental human rights? Is there a human right not to be hungry? Or are human rights themselves basic needs? Are there basic needs other than material needs which embrace human rights? Does the respect for rights and the satisfaction of needs go together, or can there be conflict?

Whatever the relation between needs and rights, they clearly are two different things. Meeting basic needs, at least physical basic needs, involves the use of scarce resources: land, labor, capital, foreign exchange, skills. Respect for human rights, in so far as they are negative rights, does not involve scarce resources. The right not to be assaulted, or not to be arbitrarily arrested, or to be permitted free expression does not absorb scarce resources. It is possible to omit doing wrong to many people, and to omit doing many wrongs to one person at the same time. The right to police protection against assault can be seen as a positive right to personal security. The negative right not to be assaulted is violated not by the government, but by the assailant.[1]

While it is congenial to some political ideologies and implicit in some versions of American liberalism to assume that "all good things go together," and that rights and needs are part of the same package, or even identical, there can be conflict between

1. See Charles Fried, *Right and Wrong* (Cambridge, Mass.: Harvard University Press, 1978), pp. 111-12.

184

rights and needs, at least on some reasonable interpretations of these concepts. Narrowly interpreted material needs can be met in ways which conflict with rights. If society were organized benevolently, like a zoo, or less benevolently, like a well-run prison, physical needs would be met at a high level, but human rights would be denied. In addition, the civil rights principle of one man, one vote might easily conflict with the satisfaction of basic needs. In a democracy in which everyone votes in his narrow, material self-interest, and there are no cross-percentile alliances, the poor will never have enough votes to enact redistribution in their favor; and if redistribution is a condition for meeting their basic needs, they will not have their needs met. The richest 49 percent of the population will always be able to overcompensate the middle swinging vote of 2 percent for not joining the poorest 49 percent in anti-poverty measures, and the rich will have more left over for themselves than had there been redistribution to the bottom 51 percent. Redistribution toward the middle, but not toward the poor, will be the result. The peacetime experience of democratic countries confirms the a priori reasoning, though the assumptions are unrealistic.[2] Thus, basic needs can be met in ways that deny human rights, and human rights can be practiced in ways that reject basic needs.

The psychololgist Abraham Maslow, who explored the hierarchy of basic needs and who stands firmly in the American liberal tradition, had this to say: "It is legitimate and fruitful to regard instinctoid basic needs and the metaneeds as rights as well as needs. This follows immediately upon granting that human beings have a right to be human in the sense that cats have a right to be cats. In order to be fully human, these need and metaneed gratifications are necessary, and may therefore be considered to be natural rights."[3] This is not a very fortunate way of making the point that "all good things go together." If being human is a fact, no rights can be inferred from it. It may, of course, be necessary that certain conditions must be met before we can fully

2. Robert Nozick, *Anarchy, State, and Utopia* (New York: Basic Books, 1974).

3. Abraham Maslow, *Motivation and Personality,* 2d ed. (New York: Harper and Row, 1970), p. xiii.

function as human beings. But again, no question of rights would arise. The function of a lawn mower is to mow lawns, but a broken-down lawn mower cannot be said to have a right to be repaired in order to become, fully and truly, a lawn mower. If, however, to be human is to aspire to an ideal (it makes sense to say "be a man!" and Nietzsche said "become what you are!" but it does not make sense to say "be a cat!" and even less "be a lawn mower!") the conditions for fulfilling this aspiration may be regarded as a right.

There is also an ambiguity between interpreting basic needs as "material preconditions" and "actual fulfillment." "I give you the toast of the Royal Economic Society, of economics and economists, who are the trustees not of civilization but of the possibility of civilization." So toasted Keynes the RES at a dinner in 1945. Substitute basic needs for civilization, and we must ask: Can or should the state actually satisfy basic needs, or should it provide only for the possibility of their satisfaction? This question is, of course, closely related to the previous one about needs and rights, for some forms of satisfaction are possible only at the expense of rights (in the zoo or the prison), and some rights are inconsistent with actual need fulfillment by the state, though not with the *possibility* of need fulfillment.

In the Middle Ages scholars enunciated a system of natural law and natural rights. Both law and rights were thought to have religious sanction and moral certitude outside the realm of purely human thought and activities. Bentham, in an attempt to debunk them, called natural rights "nonsense on stilts." More recently, the use of the term "rights" has come to imply a peculiar moral authority for the objective delineated. By calling some human aspiration a right, the objective in question has been given a moral and categorical supremacy, irrespective of the nature of the right, its appropriateness to the circumstances in which it is proclaimed, or the possibilities or costs of achieving it. The violation of a right is *always* wrong, though conflicts between rights can arise.

The American Declaration of Independence says: "We hold these truths to be self-evident; that all men are created equal; that they are endowed by their creator with certain unalienable rights; that among these are life, liberty, and the pursuit of happiness."

The use of the term "rights" in the Declaration and in many other places (including the quotation from Maslow) attempts to achieve what many since Hume have thought to be impossible—to derive an "ought" from an "is"; and more than this, to derive from the derived "ought" a "will." Man *is* human or *is* born equal; therefore he has the *right* to basic needs, life, liberty, and so forth; therefore we *will* give it to him. The drafters of the Declaration were not, of course, so foolish as to believe that all babies were in all respects the same. Implicit in their descriptive "is" was a mystical "ought." In spite of the fact that some were born larger than others, some heavier than others, some more intelligent than others, some more beautiful than others, and some richer than others, "in the sight of God" they were all equal. This is reflected in the expression "endowed by their creator." The distinction between literal equality (which in the last resort reduces to the identity of indiscernibles) and mystical equality is well known. But the extent to which the *faith* in mystical equality is reflected in *works* is one of the great controversial issues of social policy.

Of concern here is the second derivation: from "ought" to "will." At least some rights are merely objectives like other objectives: they have independent and instrumental values, their achievement confers benefits but also incurs costs, and they may therefore be subject to economic analysis.

To clarify these issues, it is necessary to draw some distinctions. Human rights cover at least four distinct areas. In the narrow sense they include the right not to be tortured or murdered. These rights apply under all governments, irrespective of their political color.

A second group consists of civil rights, or what in Anglo-Saxon countries is described as the "rule of law," in German as the *Rechtsstaat*. This group comprises the rights of citizens against their government. The rulers themselves are subject to the law. It is possible to have authoritarian states, without votes and other political rights, and yet an independent judiciary capable of acquitting people arrested by the executive. Civil rights are not consistent with totalitarian governments, which claim authority over the whole human being, but they are consistent with authoritarian governments and dictatorships.

In the third group are political rights. These enable citizens to participate in government by voting for their representatives. Representation can take many forms, of which one man, one vote is only one. Most people would regard political rights on the pattern of Western democracies as less important than human rights in the narrow sense, or than civil rights. Some of these human rights are negative, others positive.

The most controversial area is that of economic and social rights, embodied in the U.N. Universal Declaration of Human Rights and the International Covenant on Economic, Social, and Cultural Rights. These are positive rights to resources and therefore distinct from the negative rights not to have certain things done to one. The rights to universal primary education, to adequate health standards, to employment, to minimum wages and collective bargaining are completely different from the negative rights. What the U.N. Declaration asserts is that everyone has a right to benefit from the services of a full-fledged welfare state, however poor the society. It is often said nowadays that the negative, abstract, legalistic, or passive rights, such as equality before the law, must be accompanied or even preceded by the positive rights to education, health, and food. In this context it is said that the satisfaction of basic human needs should be an integral part of positively, constructively, and concretely defined human rights. In Africa there is a saying "Human rights begin with breakfast," and a song in Bertolt Brecht's "Beggars' Opera" goes: "Erst kommt das Fressen, dann kommt die Moral" (Grub first, then morality). The formulation of civil and political rights occurred in the days when the duties of the state were regarded as minimal, and the rights were intended to protect the citizen against the state. The formulation of economic and social rights has occurred in a period when the duties of the state were much more positively interpreted.

Insofar as the first three groups—human rights in the narrow sense, civil rights, and political rights—are negative rights (and

they all have large negative components) they require no resources; to refrain from certain actions does not call on resources
though opportunity costs may be involved. The fourth group—
economic and social rights—is essentially different in that it
requires substantial resources. The fourth group can be assimi-
lated into the first three by permitting the acquisition and exercise of these rights without a financial charge. We can establish
the rights to education, health, fire fighting, or parking by providing these services free, just as we can establish the rights to
freedom of speech and religion. But not only are rights to vote,
to free speech, and free assembly acquired and exercised without
financial charges, they also do not cost the community any
substantial sums. Not so with social and economic rights. It
follows that while there are duties corresponding to all rights, the
debit item on the balance sheet of providing social and economic
rights implies depriving someone else, or the same people later,
of some resources.

It is, of course, true that negative rights can involve opportunity costs; respecting these rights may preclude courses of action
which would have had benefits for others, and forgoing these
benefits is a cost that must be attributed to the rights. The
construction of a dam or a highway may be ruled out if we
respect the right not to be moved of those who live in the way.
But the existence of such opportunity costs does not detract from
the categorical character of the negative rights.

Is there then a right to survival, to a decent existence, to basic
needs? Has every human being born into this world, irrespective
of merit, ability, or available resources, the right to adequate
food, education, and medical attention? Few would assert such a
right even in rich societies such as the United States, which
would be able to provide for such rights. A formal commitment
to provide everyone with a decent existence not only would be
very expensive, but also would blunt incentives for work and
saving. In poor, developing societies such "rights" have to be
even more carefully examined.

The objection to assimilating positive social and economic
rights into negative human rights is twofold. First, one may
object on analytical grounds by pointing to the different logical

justifications of the two sets of rights. One may respect any number of negative rights of any number of people without running into contradictions—not so with positive rights. Second, one may object on practical and political grounds. The assimilation may give rise, and has in fact given rise, to an interpretation that entrenches privilege and aggravates deprivation; under the banner of implementing human rights, the "rights" of some are met at the expense of others.

Consider "the right to universal, free, elementary education" (Article 26 of the U.N. Declaration). First, the implementation of such a "right" in poor countries would be enormously expensive (see the section "Education" in chapter 6). A vastly greater share of a much smaller national cake (and budget) would have to be devoted to education, with the inevitable result that less would be left over for the implementation of other objectives, including other social and economic "rights." The premature drive to universal literacy can result in a denial of basic needs and opportunities to the mass of the people. A carefully selective and phased education program, including adult education, family education for parents, especially mothers, and children, and nonformal education, can be much more cost-effective, reduce the number of dropouts, and do more to meet basic needs.

Another illustration is the attempt to implement social security (Article 22) and the right to health and medical care (Article 25). Here the interpretation (or misinterpretation) of human rights has reinforced urban bias. It has led to training highly qualified doctors who are concentrated in towns, at the expense of auxiliary medical personnel, less expensively educated but desperately needed in the villages to teach hygiene and birth control and to cure or prevent communicable diseases. Whatever the interpretation of the right to health and medical care, the fact that its implementation involves costs must make it noncategorical, and therefore not a right.

A third area is labor rights. Labor standards applying to safety, hours, minimum wages, and collective bargaining and conventions opposing forced labor (Article 23) have often transferred inappropriate standards (for safety or minimum wages) and institutions (such as trade unions and collective bargaining) to societies in which they are detrimental to meeting basic needs. Present union aspirations were formulated after industrial revolutions had occurred and labor had become scarce. Collective bargaining, in such conditions, benefits both the workers and the community by giving an impetus to mechanization. In preindustrial societies, where the population and labor force are increasing at 2 to 3 percent a year and a large proportion of those of working age is without hope for jobs, collective bargaining and minimum wages can aggravate social inequality, unemployment, and poverty. Although parading as an implementation of a human right, these labor practices can deny satisfaction of the needs of those outside the fortunate labor aristocracy who happen to have found a job.

The correct way to look at a strategy of implementing social and economic human "rights" is to construct a time profile, showing who achieves what needs, how effectively, at what time, and at what sacrifices and costs. Premature attempts to aim at the best now may lead to sacrifices later and, in some cases, to sacrifices by others now. A more modest, partial attack on illiteracy, ill health, and unsatisfactory work standards is likely to meet needs more fully than an attempt to transfer allegedly universal principles from rich to poor countries immediately.

This point can be illustrated by Article 23(1), the "right" to employment. It is plain that there is no prospect, for a long time to come, of full employment in most developing countries. The strategic questions that arise are:

—To what extent does the employment objective conflict with other goals of policy, such as free choice of employment, more production (now or later), higher living standards, or greater independence from foreign assistance?
—To what extent can more employment now be achieved only by sacrificing employment later and vice versa? What is the preference of policymakers or of the people with respect to the time profile of employment growth?
—What social and institutional reforms are necessary to achieve higher employment? Are there serious social objections to working multiple shifts? Are trade union objectives

compatible with higher employment? What incomes policy is required to absorb additional labor and reduce the gross imbalance between urban and rural incomes?

Although negative human rights have a different status from the more positive social and economic rights, to conclude that negative rights are the only human rights may strike many people as too narrow an interpretation. They may wish to speak of violations of human rights even where all the negative rights are fully guaranteed. And they may think that these negative rights amount to little unless the integrity and dignity of the human personality is respected in a more positive way. They cannot accept a positive right to the full paraphernalia of a modern welfare state. But is there not a right to *some* share in a community's scarce resources, so as to avoid extreme deprivation? Do not all members of the human race, especially members of an organized community such as the state, have a right— certainly not to an equal share, nor, in a poor society, necessarily to adequate food, education, health, and employment—but to a fair share of the community's resources?[4]

If it is accepted that our common humanity and our membership in specific societies such as the state impose some obligations on us, the right to a fair share of the available resources would appear to be a human right, complementing the negative human rights. But it cannot be the right to the satisfaction of any need, however basic, for such a right would not take into account the scarcity of available resources and the necessity of interpersonal and intertemporal choices.

4. See Fried, *Right and Wrong,* chap. 4.

Bibliography

The word "processed" describes works that are reproduced from typescript by mimeograph, xerography, or similar means; such works may not be cataloged or commonly available through libraries, or may be subject to restricted circulation.

Abel-Smith, Brian, and Peter Townsend. *The Poor and the Poorest.* London: G. Bell and Sons, 1965.

Aristotle. *The Nicomachean Ethics.* London and New York: Everyman's Library, 1911.

Beckerman, Wilfred. *International Comparisons of Real Incomes.* Paris: Organisation for Economic Co-operation and Development, 1966.

————. *Two Cheers for the Affluent Society.* New York: St. Martin's Press, 1974.

————, ed. *Slow Growth in Britain: Causes and Consequences.* Oxford: Clarendon Press, 1979.

Benor, Daniel, and James Q. Harrison. "Agricultural Extension: The Training and Visit System." Washington, D.C.: World Bank, May 1977. Processed.

Burki, Shahid Javed. "Sectoral Priorities for Meeting Basic Needs." *Finance & Development,* vol. 17, no. 1 (March 1980), pp. 18–22.

Cassen, Robert H. "Population and Development: A Survey." *World Development,* vol. 4, nos. 10/11 (October/November 1976), pp. 785–830.

Chenery, Hollis, and others. *Redistribution with Growth.* London: Oxford University Press, 1974.

Clark, Colin. *Conditions of Economic Progress.* 3d ed. London: Macmillan, 1951.

Cleveland, Harlan. *The Third Try at World Order.* New York: Aspen Institute of Humanistic Studies and World Affairs Council of Philadelphia, 1976.

Dandekar, V. M., and Nilakantha Rath. *Poverty in India.* New Delhi: Ford Foundation, 1970.

Denison, Edward F. "Welfare Measurement and the GNP." *Survey of Current Business*, vol. 51, no. 1 (January 1971), pp. 13–16.

Development Co-operation, 1979 Review. Report by the Chairman of the Development Assistance Committee of the Organisation for Economic Co-operation and Development. November 1979.

Drewnowski, Jan, and Wolf Scott. "The Level of Living Index." Report no. 4. Geneva: United Nations Research Institute for Social Development, 1966.

Eberstadt, Nick. "Recent Declines in Fertility in Less Developed Countries." *World Development*, vol. 8, no. 1 (January 1980), pp. 37–60.

Fried, Charles. *Right and Wrong*. Cambridge, Mass.: Harvard University Press, 1978.

Government of India, Planning Commission. *Draft Five Year Plan, 1978–83*. Vol. 1. New Delhi, 1978.

Government of Indonesia. *Repelita III: The Third Five Year Development Plan, 1979–84*. English translation. Jakarta, 1979.

Government of Kenya. *Development Plan, 1979–1983*. Nairobi, 1978.

Government of the Philippines. *Five Year Philippine Development Plan, 1978–82*. Manila, 1977.

Gross, Daniel R., and Barbara A. Underwood. "Technological Change and Caloric Costs: Sisal Agriculture in Northeastern Brazil." *American Anthropologist*, vol. 73, no. 3 (June 1971), pp. 725–40.

Harberger, Arnold C. "On the Use of Distributional Weights in Social Cost-Benefit Analysis." Paper presented at a conference on Research in Taxation sponsored by the National Science Foundation and the National Bureau of Economic Research, Stanford, California, January 1976. Supplement to *Journal of Political Economy*, vol. 86, no. 2, pt. 2, (April 1978), pp. S87–S120.

Harris, John R., and Michael P. Todaro. "Migration, Unemployment and Development: A Two-Sector Analysis." *American Economic Review*, vol. 60, no. 1 (March 1970), pp. 126–42.

Heath, Edward. "The Way to Avoid a Caribbean Crisis." *The* (London) *Times*, March 12, 1980.

Hicks, Norman L. "Basic Needs and the New International Economic Order." Background paper for *World Development Report, 1980*. Washington, D.C.: World Bank, 1979. Processed.

———. "Sector Priorities in Meeting Basic Needs: Some Statistical Evidence." Washington, D.C.: World Bank, 1979. Processed.

————. "Growth versus Basic Needs: Is There a Trade-off?" *World Development*, vol. 7, no. 11/12 (November/December 1979), pp. 985–94.

————. "Is There a Trade-Off between Growth and Basic Needs?" *Finance & Development*, vol. 17, no. 2 (June 1980), pp. 17–20.

Hirschman, Albert O. *Journeys Toward Progress*. New York: Twentieth Century Fund, 1963.

International Labour Organisation ILO. *Employment, Growth and Basic Needs: A One-World Problem*. Geneva, 1976.

Isenman, Paul. "Basic Needs: The Case of Sri Lanka." *World Development*, vol. 8, no. 3 (March 1980), pp. 237–58.

Johnston, B. F., and William Clark. "Food, Health and Population: Policy Analysis and Development Priorities in Low-Income Countries." Working Paper no. 79-52. Laxenburg, Austria: International Institute for Applied Systems Analysis, 1979.

Johnston, B. F., and A. J. Meyer. "Nutrition, Health and Population in Strategies for Rural Development." *Economic Development and Cultural Change*, vol., 26, no. 1 (October 1977), pp. 1–23.

Knight, Peter T., and others. "Brazil: Human Resources Special Report." Washington, D.C.: World Bank, 1979. Processed.

Kravis, Irving B., Alan Heston, and Robert Summers. *International Comparisons of Real Product and Purchasing Power*. Baltimore, Md.: Johns Hopkins University Press, 1978.

Kravis, Irving B., Zoltan Kenessey, Alan Heston, and Robert Summers. *A System of International Comparisons of Gross Product and Purchasing Power*. Baltimore, Md.: Johns Hopkins University Press, 1975.

Kuznets, Simon. "Economic Growth and Income Inequality." *American Economic Review*, vol. 45, no. 1 (March 1955), pp. 1–28.

————. "Quantitative Aspects of Economic Growth of Nations," VIII: Distribution of Income by Size," *Economic Development and Cultural Change*, vol. 11, no. 2, pt. 2 (January 1963), pp. 1–80.

————. "Problems in Comparing Recent Growth Rates for Developed and Less Developed Countries." *Economic Development and Cultural Change*, vol. 20, no. 2 (January 1972), pp. 185–209.

Leibenstein, Harvey. "A Branch of Economics is Missing: Micro-Micro Theory." *Journal of Economic Literature*, vol. 17, no. 2 (June 1979), pp. 477–502.

Lewis, W. A. "Economic Development with Unlimited Supplies of Labour." *Manchester School of Economics and Social Studies,* vol. 22, no. 2 (May 1954), pp. 139-91.

———. *The Theory of Economic Growth.* London: Allen and Unwin, 1955.

Marx, Karl, and Frederick Engels. *Selected Works.* Vol. 1. Moscow: Foreign Languages Publishing House, 1958.

Maslow, Abraham. *Motivation and Personality.* 2d ed. New York: Harper and Row, 1970.

McGranahan, D. V., Claude Richaud-Proust, N. V. Sovani, and Muthu Subramanian. *Contents and Measurement of Socio-Economic Development.* New York: Praeger, 1972.

Morawetz, David. *Twenty-five Years of Economic Development: 1950 to 1975.* Baltimore, Md.: Johns Hopkins University Press, 1977.

———. "Basic Needs Policies and Population Growth." *World Development,* vol. 6, no. 11/12 (November/December 1978), pp. 1251–59.

Morris, M. D., and F. B. Liser. "The PQLI: Measuring Progress in Meeting Human Needs." Communique on Development Issues no. 32. Washington, D.C.: Overseas Development Council, 1977.

Mott, Frank L., and Susan Mott. "Kenya's Record Population Growth: A Dilemma of Development." *Population Bulletin,* vol. 55, no. 5 (October 1980), pp. 785-830.

Myrdal, Gunnar. *Asian Drama: An Inquiry into the Poverty of Nations.* New York: Twentieth Century Fund, 1968.

Nepal, National Planning Commission Secretariat. *Basic Principles of Sixth Plan, 1980–85.* Katmandu, April 1979.

Nordhaus, William D., and James Tobin. "Is Growth Obsolete?" In *Economic Growth.* New York: Columbia University Press for National Bureau for Economic Research, 1972.

Nozick, Robert. *Anarchy, State and Utopia.* New York: Basic Books, 1974.

Organisation for Economic Co-operation and Development (OECD), Development Assistance Committee. "Performance Compendium: Consolidated Results of Analytical Work on Economic and Social Performance of Developing Countries." Paris, 1973.

———. "Socio-economic Typologies or Criteria and Their Usefulness in Measuring Development Progress." Paris, April 7, 1977.

Pant, Pitambar. "Perspective of Development, India 1960-61 to 1975-76: Implications of Planning for a Minimum Level of Living." In

Poverty and Income Distribution in India. Edited by T. N. Srinivasan and P. K. Bardhan. Calcutta: Statistical Publishing Society, 1974.

Perkins, Dwight. "Rural Health in China." Washington, D.C.: World Bank, 1979 Processed.

Pigou, A. C. *The Economics of Welfare.* 1st ed. London: Macmillan, 1920.

Provisional Military Government of Socialist Ethiopia. *First Year Programme of the National Revolutionary Development Campaign.* May 1979.

Pyatt, Graham, and Jeffery Round. "Social Accounting Matrices for Development Planning." *Review of Income and Wealth,* ser. 23, no. 4 (December 1977), pp. 339–64.

Rawls, John. *The Theory of Justice.* Cambridge, Mass. Harvard University Press, 1971.

Reutlinger, Shlomo, and Marcelo Selowsky. *Malnutrition and Poverty: Magnitude and Policy Options.* Baltimore, Md.: Johns Hopkins University Press, 1976.

Rowntree, B. Seebohm, *Poverty: A Study of Town Life.* London: Macmillan, 1901.

Scitovsky, Tibor. *The Joyless Economy.* New York: Oxford University Press, 1976.

Scrimshaw, Susan C. M. "Infant Mortality and Behavior in the Regulation of Family Size." *Population and Development Review,* vol. 4, no. 3 (September 1978), pp. 383–403.

Seers, Dudley. "Life Expectancy as an Integrating Concept in Social and Demographic Analysis and Planning." *Review of Income and Wealth,* ser. 23, no. 3 (September 1977), pp. 195–203.

Sen, A. K. "Economic Development: Objectives and Obstacles." Paper presented at the Research Conference on the Lessons of China's Development Experience for the Developing Countries. Sponsored by the Social Science Research Council/American Council of Learned Societies, Joint Committee on Contemporary China, San Juan, Puerto Rico, 1976.

———. "Poverty: An Ordinal Approach to Measurement." *Econometrica,* vol. 44, no. 2 (March 1976), pp. 219-31.

———. *Poverty and Economic Development.* Second Vikram Sarabhai Memorial Lecture. Ahmedabad, December 5, 1976.

———. *Three Notes on the Concept of Poverty.* World Employment Programme Research Working Paper, WEP2-23/WP65. Geneva: International Labour Office. 1978.

————. "Ethical Issues in Income Distribution: National and International." Paper presented to the symposium on the Past and Prospects of the Economic World Order, Saltsjöbaden, Sweden, August 1978.

————. "The Welfare Basis of Real Income Comparisons: A Survey." *Journal of Economic Literature*, vol. 17, no. 1 (March 1979), pp. 1–45.

Sheehan, Glen, and Michael Hopkins. *Basic Needs Performance: An Analysis of Some International Data.* World Employment Programme Research Working Paper, WEP2–23/WP9. Geneva: International Labour Office, 1978.

Singer, H. W. "Poverty, Income Distribution and Levels of Living: Thirty Years of Changing Thought on Development Problems." In *Reflections on Economic Development and Social Change: Essays in Honour of Professor V. K. R. V. Rao.* Edited by C. H. Hanumantha Rao and P. C. Joshi. Bombay: Allied Publishers Private Ltd.; 1979; and Delhi: Institute of Economic Growth, 1979.

Singh, Ajit. "The 'Basic Needs' Approach to Development vs. the New International Economic Order: The Significance of Third World Industrialization." *World Development,* vol. 7, no. 6 (June 1979), pp. 585–606.

Singh, Ajit, and Manfred Bienefeld. "Industry and Urban Economy in Tanzania." Background paper for the ILO, Jobs and Skills Programme for Africa, Employment Advisory Mission to Tanzania. Addis Ababa, circa 1977. Processed.

Sinha, Radha, Peter Pearson, Gopal Kadekodi, and Mary Gregory. *Income Distribution, Growth and Basic Needs in India.* London: Croom Helm, 1979.

Sivard, Ruth. "World Military and Social Expenditures, 1979." Leesburg, Va.: World Priorities, 1979.

Smith, Adam. *The Wealth of Nations.* Edited by Edwin Cannan. 3d ed. London: Methuen, 1922.

Srinivasan, T. N. "Development, Poverty, and Basic Human Needs: Some Issues." *Food Research Institute Studies.* vol. 16, no. 2 (1977), pp. 11–28.

Stewart, Frances. "Country Experience in Providing for Basic Needs." *Finance and Development,* vol. 16, no. 4 (December 1979), pp. 23–26.

Stone, Richard. *Toward a System of Social and Demographic Statistics.* New York: United Nations, 1975.

Streeten, Paul. "Industrialization in a Unified Development Strategy." *World Development,* vol. 3, no. 1 (January 1975), pp. 1–9.

Streeten, Paul, and Shahid Javed Burki. "Basic Needs: Some Issues." *World Development*, vol. 6, no. 3 (March 1978), pp. 411–21.

Sukhatme, P. V. *Malnutrition and Poverty*. Ninth Lal Bahadur Shastri Memorial Lecture, January 29, 1977. New Delhi: Indian Agricultural Research Institute, 1977.

Terleckyj, Nestor, *Improvements in the Quality of Life*. Washington, D.C.: National Planning Association, 1975.

Townsend, Peter. *Poverty in the United Kingdom: A Survey of Household Resources and Standards of Living*. Berkeley and Los Angeles: University of California Press, 1979.

United Nations. *Poverty, Unemployment and Development Policy: A Case Study of Selected Issues with Reference to Kerala*. ST/ESA/29. New York, 1975.

United Nations, Economic and Social Council (ECOSOC), Committee for Development Planning. "Developing Countries and Levels of Development." New York, October 15, 1975.

United Nations Educational, Scientific and Cultural Organization (Unesco). *The Use of Socio-Economic Indicators in Development Planning*. Paris, 1976.

United Nations General Assembly. A/AC. 191/21. New York, April 28, 1978.

United States, Agency for International Development (USAID). "Socioeconomic Performance Criteria for Development." Washington, D.C., February 1977.

Wheeler, David. "Basic Needs Fulfillment and Economic Growth: A Simultaneous Model." *Journal of Development Economics*, vol. 7, no. 4 (December 1980), pp. 435–51.

World Bank. *World Development Report, 1979*. New York: Oxford University Press, 1979.

―――. *World Development Report, 1980*. New York: Oxford University Press, 1980.

Index

Abel-Smith, Brian, 19n

Administrative skills, as requirement for basic needs, 41, 51–53, 148–49

Afghanistan: education in, 136; life expectancy in, 113

Africa, 119–20; education in, 138; employment in, 14; growth of, 32; income per capita in, 11; life expectancy in, 130; literacy in, 119–20

Ahluwalia, Montek S., 73, 106

Angola, life expectancy in, 113

Argentina: growth in, 32; life expectancy in, 113

Aristotle, 18

Asia: education in, 138; income per capita in, 11; life expectancy in, 130

Bangladesh, growth in, 32

Basic needs, 4–7, 21–23; administration and, 51–53, 148–49; as approach, 32–45; conflicts with, 179–83; cost of, 51–52, 174–75; definition of, 32–33, 61, 72–73, 123–45; determination of, 25–26; government interventions and, 41–45, 112; vs. growth, 96–108, 174; implementation of, 27–28, 46–67; as integrating concept, 23–25; international assistance and, 112, 168, 174–76; interpretations of, 25–28, 168–69, 180–81; sectoral linkages and, 47–51, 152–55; objectives of, 3; opposition to, 180–83; politics and, 26–27; sectoral priorities and, 154–61; program for, 112; as strategy, 8, 9, 64–65; systemic change and, 112; technologies and, 51–53; waste and, 38. *See also* Needs, non–basic

Beckerman, Wilfred, 17, 80n

Benor, Daniel, 153–54

Bhutan, life expectancy in, 113

Bienefeld, Manfred, 101n

Brazil: basic needs expenditures in, 97; growth in, 31–32, 98–99, 107, 120–22; health care in, 132; sectoral linkages in, 153–55; malnutrition in, 61, 152

British Medical Research Council, 155

Burki, Shahid Javed, 92n, 123n

Burma: consumption in, 100; growth in, 103; life expectancy in, 103, 116

Cassen, Robert H., 39n, 52n

Chad, life expectancy in, 113

Chenery, Hollis, 15n, 53n, 73, 106

China, 115; basic needs in, 61, 117; growth in, 31–32; income per capita in, 11; life expectancy in, 116; mortality in, 117; participation in, 62; political regime of, 56

Clark, Colin, 70

Clark, William, 153n

Cleveland, Harlan, 179n

Colombia: basic needs expenditures in, 97; employment in, 12; growth in, 31; inequality in, 31

The full range of World Bank publications, both free and for sale, is described in the *Catalog of World Bank Publications*; the continuing research program is outlined in *World Bank Research Program: Abstracts of Current Studies*. Both booklets are updated annually; the most recent edition of each is available without charge from the Publications Unit, World Bank, 1818 H Street, N.W., Washington, D.C. 20433, U.S.A.

Paul Streeten is director of the Center for Asian Development Studies at Boston University, editor of *World Development*, and a consultant to the World Bank. Shahid Javed Burki is senior economic and policy adviser in External Relations at the World Bank. Mahbub ul Haq is director of Policy Planning and Program Review at the World Bank, and Norman Hicks is senior economist in the same department. Frances Stewart is a fellow of Somerville College, Oxford University, senior research officer at the Institute of Commonwealth Studies, and a former World Bank consultant.